DEMOS

D1485063

Demos is an independent think tank committed to new thinking on the long term problems facing the UK and other advanced industrial societies.

It aims to develop ideas – both theoretical and practical – to help shape the politics of the 21st century, and to improve the breadth and quality of political debate.

Demos publishes books and a quarterly journal and undertakes substantial empirical and policy oriented research projects. Demos is a registered charity.

In all its work Demos brings together people from a wide range of backgrounds in business, academia, government, the voluntary sector and the media to share and cross-fertilise ideas and experiences.

For further information and
subscription details please write to:
Demos
9 Bridewell Place
London, EC4V 6AP
Telephone: 0171 353 4479
Facsimile: 0171 353 4481
email: mail@demos.co.uk

The Rise of the Social Entrepreneur

Charles Leadbeater

DEM●S

First published in 1997 by
Demos
9 Bridewell Place
London EC4V 6AP
Telephone: 0171 353 4479
Facsimile: 0171 353 4481
e-mail: mail@demos.co.uk
© Demos 1997

Paper No. 25
ISBN 1 898309 53 1
Printed in Great Britain by
Lasting Impressions Limited
Designed by Esterson Lackersteen
Typeset by Lindsay Nash
Photographs by Guy Drayton
Production by Royal SunAlliance Creative Print Services
Thanks to Adrian Taylor

Contents

Acknowledgments

I would like to thank NatWest Bank and Royal SunAlliance for funding the research for this report in the Autumn of 1996. Victoria Ward, at NatWest Capital Markets, was particularly helpful and provided extensive comments on an early draft. Libby Brayshaw at Royal SunAlliance provided great support. Geoff Mulgan, Geraldine Bedell, and Ian Hargreaves all provided helpful comments on an early draft. Tom Bentley not only commented on my drafts but has also been invaluable in organising the publication and presentation of the report. I would also like to thank all the five entrepreneurs whose work forms the basis of the report and who gave up a great deal of time to help me. Of course any errors of fact or judgement are my responsibility.

Charles Leadbeater
January 1997

Executive summary

1. The welfare state was designed for a world of male full employment and stable families which no longer exists. The interlocking system of macroeconomic policies, state social insurance schemes and tax financed services is under increasing pressure, unable to respond effectively to a growing array of social problems – mass long term joblessness, drugs, family break-up, illiteracy.

2. Although criticism of the welfare state is mounting, radical reform is still controversial and highly contested. Resistance to paying more taxes for welfare does not mean people support a dismantling of the social safety net. As a result reforms have mainly focused on cost cutting and gradually reducing entitlements to benefits.

3. As a society we are stuck in an impasse. We have a welfare state system which we know is ill-equipped to deal with many of the modern social problems it has to confront. Yet we are unable to sanction radical reforms to make welfare more affordable and more effective.

4. We need a different approach to break through this impasse. Britain needs a long wave of social innovation to develop a new philosophy, practice and organisation of welfare. This wave of innovation must develop a problem solving welfare system, to gradually take over from the current system which often simply maintains people in a state of dependency and poverty. It must be an active welfare system designed to create social capital by encouraging people to take greater control over their lives.

5. This wave of social innovation will come from several sources. Innovation in ideas and policies will be vital to underpin the values and philosophy of an active, problem-solving welfare system. Organisational innovation will also be important, to create new institutions capable of delivering a new form of welfare.

6. Social entrepreneurs will be one of the most important sources of innovation. Social entrepreneurs identify under-utilised resources – people, buildings, equipment – and find ways of putting them to use to satisfy unmet social needs. They innovate new welfare services and new ways of delivering existing services. Social entrepreneurs who deploy entrepreneurial skills for social ends are at work in parts of the traditional public sector, some large private sector corporations and at the innovative edge of the voluntary sector.

7. This report is based on case studies of five social entrepreneurs. Helen Taylor-Thompson is the motive force at the Mildmay Mission Hospital, a Victorian hospital closed by the NHS in 1984 which she helped to turn into one of the world's leading centres for Aids care. Andrew Mawson has created a thriving centre in Bromley-by-Bow from a church that was on its knees a decade ago. Adele Blakebrough, a Baptist minister, runs one of the most innovative drug treatment programmes in the country from a church in Kingston, south London. Tony McGann started a tenants' co-operative in the early 1980s and has turned it into an award winning housing scheme, with 300 houses near the centre of Liverpool. Geoff Thompson's Youth Charter for Sport is brokering relationships between sporting celebrities and major corporations to support sporting schemes which encourage young people on depressed estates away from drugs and crime.

8. Social entrepreneurs are driven, ambitious leaders, with great skills in communicating a mission and inspiring staff, users and partners. In all these cases they have been capable of creating impressive schemes with virtually no resources.

9. Social entrepreneurs create flat and flexible organisations, with a core of full time paid staff, which work with few resources but a culture of creativity.

10. These organisations all operate in complex, multi-agency environments where several arms of the state as well as distinct groups of professionals are all seeking to address an issue. Social entrepreneurs often find ways of combining approaches which are traditionally kept separate.

11. Socially entrepreneurial organisations generally have an open and porous approach to their environment. They do not see themselves as providing their clients with a specific service; their aim is to form long term relationships with their users which develop over time. These organisations are inclusive, they create a sense of membership by recognising that their users all have distinct and different needs.

12. The work of social entrepreneurs creates value in several ways. They operate as a kind of research and development wing of the welfare system, innovating new solutions to intractable social problems. They often deliver services far more efficiently than the public sector. Most importantly they set in motion a virtuous circle of social capital accumulation. They help communities to build up social capital which gives them a better chance of standing on their own feet.

13. If Britain is to develop a more effective and affordable problem-solving welfare system we have to support social innovation. One of the best ways to do that is to support the work of social entrepreneurs both within and outside the public sector. We recommend a series of measures government could take to promote social entrepreneurship:

● Support the '2,000 by 2,000' initiative to create 2,000 social entrepreneurs by the Millennium. This would form the basis for a social entrepreneurs' self-help network, linked by an Intranet.

● Fund research into the feasibility of creating a Centre for Social Entrepreneurship, a kind of business school for social entrepreneurs, which would service social entrepreneurs from the public, private and voluntary sectors.

● Help to create local welfare networks to bring together education establishments, social schemes, health schemes and employment and enterprise schemes within a locality.

● Create a Lessons Learned Unit for the public sector which would collect, interpret and disseminate examples of best practice in public management and social innovation.

● Simplify the legal structures for social organisations by creating a simple, de-regulated, off-the-shelf legal form which these organisations could adopt.

● Business in the Community and leading companies involved in community programmes should explore ways to form more strategic, lasting partnerships with social entrepreneurs involving twinning agreements, mentoring and staff exchanges.

● The government should identify perhaps 100 social entrepreneurs around the country whose organisations could act as a test bed for new policy proposals and ideas.
● Ensure that the Department of Trade and Industry includes social entrepreneurs within its programmes to help small and medium sized businesses.

14. This Demos report will form the basis for a rolling programme of seminars and conferences to promote the concept of social entrepreneurship.

Introduction

How to get something from nothing

Andrew Mawson arrived in Bromley-by-Bow, one of Britain's most depressed districts, in 1984, as the newly appointed minister at a United Reformed church which was on its last legs. The church hall had a leaking roof, a central heating system that barely worked, a piano so old that the keys were stuck together and a congregation of a few elderly parishioners. Mawson persuaded his ageing congregation that the only way the church could respond to the mounting social crisis of unemployment, illiteracy and ill health in the neighbourhood was by putting the church's facilities completely at the disposal of local people.

This strategy of openness has produced a remarkable transformation. The once cold and leaking church has been refurbished and opened out to serve as a nursery and creche during the week and a sacramental centre in the evenings and at the weekend. The adjacent hall is thriving with activity, ranging from a large community care programme to a set of artists' workshops for local people.

The centre is the base for a literacy outreach programme for 300 local Bengali families. The staff, volunteers and centre members, usually eat lunch in a self-financing cafe, attached to the building. A health centre, which the centre says is the first in Britain to be owned by its patients, is about to be opened after an investment of more than £1 million in a stylishly designed building. The Royal SunAlliance insurance group is financing a £300,000, three year project to create new ways of diverting young people away from crime. NatWest Bank has just awarded the centre £220,000 for a three year scheme to promote young local entrepreneurs. The adjacent park, which houses the centre, is being redesigned with a series of sculptures. Plans are afoot to create housing for single homeless people and an enterprise centre for local businesses. Out of nothing has emerged a thriving centre which combines health and welfare with work and enterprise, serving young and old, black and white, pulling together resources from the local and central state, the private sector and the church. Everything has been done to the highest possible standards. The centre is driven by a powerful ethic of creativity, excellence and achievement. The Bromley-by-Bow Centre is an inspiring example of social entrepreneurship. It is far from the only one.

Take the story of Helen Taylor-Thompson and the Mildmay Mission Hospital in Shoreditch, east London. In 1982 the Mildmay, a district general hospital, was due to close in the rationalisation of NHS services in the area. Helen Taylor-Thompson, who had been involved with the hospital for 30 years, was determined it would not shut. After a long campaign she persuaded the government to allow the hospital to re-open by leaving the NHS and leasing the buildings on a peppercorn rent.

By 1996 the Mildmay had become one of the world's leading centres for Aids care, with an international reputation for innovation. In 1988 it became the first Aids hospice in Europe. It has 32 suites for the terminal care of people with Aids housed in the old Victorian hospital. In addition it has a purpose built facility to treat parents with Aids, without separating them from their children. The Mildmay's reputation is international. This year it plans to open a treatment centre in Kampala, Uganda. It has provided consultancy and advice to eleven other countries. Mildmay is a world class institution created from a hospital that was regarded as worthless a decade ago.

Helen Taylor-Thompson is not alone in being virtually written off by the public sector. It's an experience that Eric Blakebrough knows all too well. When he became the minister at the Baptist Church in Kingston, south London, in 1968, almost his first act was to set up a club for young people to visit after the pubs had shut. It was through his open, non-judgmental engagement with young people that Blakebrough came to understand the extent to which some of them were dependent on drugs and had untreated health problems.

Out of that beginning has grown one of the most innovative and effective drug treatment programmes in the country, run by Eric's daughter Adele, who has taken over both the ministry and the project. About 300 people a day visit the project for a dose of methadone, designed to help them come off heroin. Successive studies have demonstrated that Kaleidoscope is both more effective and efficient than comparable public sector programmes. A hostel next to the church provides long-stay accommodation for nineteen single young people. In two adjacent houses are a library, a computer room, music and art workshops and an education and enterprise centre. Plans have been drawn up to build an intensive care unit and cafeteria on land nearby.

Kaleidoscope is almost 30 years old. It is a mature organisation. Geoff Thompson is at the other end of the process. His organisation, The Youth Charter for Sport, has only just been born. In 1992 Thompson, a former karate world champion and by then a member of the Sports Council, was part of the team working on Manchester's bid to host the Olympics in the year 2000. Two drug related shootings in Manchester's Moss Side convinced him that the private and public sectors were unable effectively to respond to what he regarded as the sense of social anarchy among young people on the city's depressed housing estates. As he puts it: 'No square mile in the country has had more public money pumped into it to less effect than Moss Side and Hulme.'

Thompson's frustration with the inadequacies of the official response led him to create the Youth Charter for Sport in 1993. The idea is simple: Thompson will use the attraction of sporting celebrities to bring together private sector sponsors and schemes to provide sporting opportunities for disadvantaged young people who regard sporting celebrities as their role models. Sport provides one of the few bridges between young people and the corporate sector; both have an intense interest in being associated with sporting celebrity. Thompson hopes to create a network of Youth Charter for Sport offices around the country to act as brokers, bringing together local sporting celebrities, corporate sponsors and schemes designed to encourage young people away from drugs and crime.

Tony McGann started from beginnings as small as Geoff Thompson's. McGann was a community housing activist in the Vauxhall area of Liverpool in the 1970s at a time when traditional working class communities were being broken up. Manufacturing jobs were disappearing down the sink and the council was re-housing people in peripheral modern estates on the outskirts of the city. McGann brought together tenants in one tenement block on Eldon Street. They formed a co-operative and insisted they were staying put.

That co-operative was the source for one of the most impressive housing and community regeneration schemes in the country. The Eldonian housing association has built 300 high quality homes, with more on the way. Tenants were involved in the design of all the houses. The Eldonians say the estate is crime-free. It has a nursery, sports facilities and job training programmes.

Andrew Mawson, Helen Taylor-Thompson, Eric and Adele Blakebrough, Geoff Thompson and Tony McGann represent a new breed of social entrepreneur. These social

15

entrepreneurs are creating innovative ways of tackling some of our most pressing and intractable social problems: youth crime, drugs dependency, chronic joblessness, illiteracy, Aids and mental illness. They take under-utilised and often discarded resources – people and buildings – and re-energise them by finding new ways to use them which satisfy unmet and often unrecognised needs.

The five organisations which form of the core of this report run inspiring, transformatory projects. Their potential and significance extends well beyond their particular projects. The entrepreneurialism, innovation, creativity and dynamism of these projects shows how we could promote a modern type of social welfare for the 21st century. These schemes mobilise people to tackle social problems collaboratively. They are caring and compassionate but professional and business-like. They set high expectations and standards. They demand a lot of their users and clients. They bridge the gap between the private and public sectors, the state and the market, to develop effective and efficient solutions to our most complex and pressing social problems.

In the post-war era the growth of the welfare state was seen by most people as a symbol of social progress. No more. The welfare state is widely criticised for being inflexible, slow moving, bureaucratic, de-humanising and disempowering. We will only make social progress if we overcome division and exclusion by restoring a sense of social cohesion. A modern mobile society will only cohere if we are prepared to innovate with new ways of delivering welfare. That is what social entrepreneurs do. That is why they are so important.

There is a growing political and intellectual consensus that we need to start looking beyond the confines of the traditional welfare state and the voluntary sector for solutions to our social ills. The Liberals have long supported a form of community politics which encourages local regeneration initiatives. The Conservatives have been most critical of the shortcomings of the welfare state. A notion of active citizenship is central to the self styled civic Conservatism espoused by the centre of the latter day Tory party. Labour, which in many ways is the party most committed to the traditional welfare state, is starting to recognise the case for reform and innovation as it confronts the constraints on public spending.

All these currents are leading in the same direction. Britain's tradition of welfare cannot be dismantled, it must be modernised. That modernisation will only be successful with innovation and entrepreneurship to create new forms of welfare. Some of that innovation will come from new ideas and policies. But ideas will not work unless they can be translated into practice by organisational and institutional innovation at the sharp end of welfare provision. We must use both blades of the scissors: new institutions and new ideas. The social entrepreneurs who will carry new ideas into practice will come from three main sources.

First, there is a growing body of innovation within the public sector, encouraged by contracting-out, local management of schools and devolution of power within the NHS. This is encouraging public sector managers and workers to find new ways of delivering welfare services.

Second, the private sector is showing a growing interest in the social setting for business, particularly the quality of education. This should promote a cross-pollination of entrepreneurial practices from the private sector into areas of welfare.

Third, the voluntary sector is developing an innovative leading edge which is the most fertile source of social entrepreneurship. Social entrepreneurs are emerging from often small organisations, deploying business skills in social settings.

It is from the conjunction of these three forces (set out in Figure 1 overleaf) that social innovation will emerge.

Figure 1. Sources of social entrepreneurship

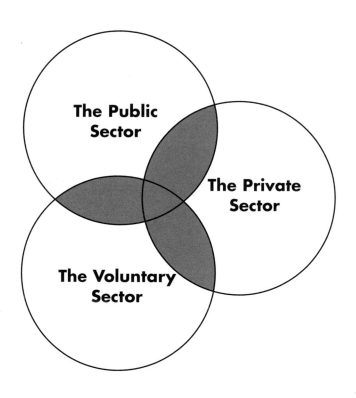

The Public
Sector

The Private
Sector

The Voluntary
Sector

The Social
Entrepreneurs'
Sector

What is a social entrepreneur?

At first sight the idea of social entrepreneurship might seem paradoxical. Entrepreneurs are hero figures in the profit-seeking private sector. How can social welfare and entrepreneurship be brought together? The best place to start is by defining the two components of the idea: the social and the entrepreneur.

The social

The entrepreneurs studied in this report are social in several senses.

- Their output is social: they promote health, welfare and well-being.
- Their core assets are forms of social capital – relationships, networks, trust and co-operation – which give them access to physical and financial capital.
- The organisations they found are social, in the sense that they are not owned by shareholders and do not pursue profit as their main objective. These organisations are social also in the sense that they are part of civil society, rather than the state. Indeed they are innovative often because they are at odds with the central and local state.
- Social entrepreneurs are often community entrepreneurs, attempting to regenerate the locality, estate or neighbourhood in which they are based. However not all social entrepreneurs are based in geographically defined communities. Many serve wider constituencies: Mildmay Hospital serves an international constituency concerned with the care of people with Aids; Geoff Thompson's aim is to serve young people throughout Britain, not just in Manchester.

The entrepreneur

People such as Andrew Mawson, Adele Blakebrough, Helen Taylor-Thompson, Geoff Thompson and Tony McGann share many of the characteristics which typify entrepreneurs in all walks of life.

- They excel at spotting unmet needs and mobilise under-utilised resources to meet these needs.

- They are driven and determined, ambitious and charismatic. Social entrepreneurs are driven by a mission, rather than by the pursuit of profit or shareholder value.
- In the private sector it is quite possible to be a successful entrepreneur without being at all innovative. In the social sector it is far more likely that an entrepreneur will also be an innovator. The people highlighted in this report are entrepreneurial because they are innovative: they develop new services and organisations.

Social entrepreneurs are most usually found in what is called the voluntary sector. Yet this description can be misleading. Certainly they run not-for-profit organisations, which rely on a great deal of voluntary help and effort. Yet they are also distinguished by a professionalism and dynamism most commonly seen in small, fast growing businesses. Much of the voluntary sector is slow moving and specialist: that is one of its strengths. Voluntary organisations can be innovative but many also operate with a very fixed idea of their clients' needs.

But social entrepreneurs increasingly are not confined to voluntary organisations. As the welfare state becomes more decentralised with the spread of a contract culture, there will be more room for experimentation and diversity. Large private sector companies may also become involved in social innovation, through partnerships with voluntary organisations and a growing role in the provision of education and social insurance. Large private sector companies will find they need entrepreneurs who can bring together commercial and social needs.

Innovation in all forms – organisational, technological and social – is becoming ever more vital to the long term health of the economy. Social innovation will be particularly important for two reasons.

The first is that we need to innovate to respond more effectively to a range of social problems which the welfare state is ill-equipped, as it stands, to tackle. At the risk of caricaturing its complex beginnings, the welfare state was designed for a post-war world of male full-employment, stable families and low female employment. Those underpinnings have been destroyed by international competition and social change. New social problems of single parent households, drug dependency and long term unemployment have emerged with which the traditional welfare system is not designed to deal. We need to innovate new responses to the new social and economic realities.

The second reason is economic. All societies with developed welfare systems are slowly chipping away at historic welfare entitlements, in an attempt to cut the costs of welfare. A much more radical overhaul of welfare provision is required if the burden of the welfare state on the economy is to be reduced significantly. Innovation is the only hope we have of maintaining the quality of welfare while reducing its costs. A more innovative, efficient welfare system should make more of a contribution to the economic health of society as a whole.

The argument of this report is that social entrepreneurs are the most likely sources of workable innovations. The voluntary sector, with a turnover of about £11.6 billion a year, already accounts for about 10 per cent of all service sector employment. The voluntary sector already provides a majority of pre-school day care for under-fives, as well as substantial amounts of care for the elderly, primary education and housing. Its scope for growth in other areas of welfare provision, such as secondary education, health and even social security and legal services, could be significant.

The big question is whether social entrepreneurs have the skills and resources to take on a much larger role in providing social welfare, in alliance with the public sector and private companies. This report has three main aims:
● to explain why we need a wave of social innovation led by social entrepreneurs
● to explain how entrepreneurial social organisations are created and developed
● to recommend some practical steps the government, companies and social entrepreneurs should take to set in motion a wave of welfare innovation.

The setting

The search for the public good and the decline of the welfare state

We are growing less confident of our ability to sustain social cohesion and maintain shared values in a society which is becoming more diverse and divided.

We live in an anti-hierarchical age, in which deference to traditional sources of authority – the social order of class, the churches, the traditional family – is in decline. The ethic of individual self-fulfilment and achievement is the most powerful current in modern society. The choosing, deciding, shaping individual who aspires to be the author of their life, the creator of their identity, free within their private sphere, is the central character of our times. For many people social progress is measured by the expansion of individual choice within this private sphere. This individualism is not just consumerist. It is also moral. In many ways this is a more moral time than in the 1950s and 1960s. Young people these days feel more passionately and morally about a wider range of issues than they used to – from our treatment of the environment and animals, to gender, race and human rights around the world. People are more likely to challenge the right of established figures of authority to lay down the moral law. For many people, especially young people, arguments that we need to rebuild a sense of community to restore a sense of social order and discipline will either seem cynical, hypocritical, sentimental or coercive. Any attempt to restore a sense of social cohesion has to start from a recognition that diversity, scepticism and individualism are written into our culture.

But that does not mean we should not try nor that people do not want a sense of social security and belonging. They do. They do not want it on the nostalgic, backward looking terms offered to them by most politicians. The task which confronts all of us in different ways is how to create a modern sense of society and cohesion. The starting point for that, and many of the schemes profiled in this report, is the yawning gap between the global scale of modern economic life and the intimate terms in which people conceive their identities and make their choices, in neighbourhoods, families, networks of friends, churches. That gap is disorienting: our plans, hopes, dreams, our sense of control over our lives can suddenly be uprooted by forces out beyond our reach. In times which seem increasingly rootless, a sense of community is both more desired and yet more distant. Identities cannot be created out of thin air, even in these fluid times. They come from the interplay of personal histories with larger traditions and communities. Take away communities and you take away the civic values they give us. Individual lives make little sense if they are completely separated from shared ventures.

As a society we encourage individuals to articulate their interests, their distinctive sense of themselves. Acquiring a sense of yourself is vital to fulfilment. Yet we have not matched our ability to articulate our differences with institutions through which we can negotiate and reconcile these competing and conflicting interests. It is this imbalance between our ability to articulate differences and our ability to reconcile them, that accounts for our lack of confidence in defining a shared sense of the public good.

Where should we look for a modern, vibrant sense of the public good? It is unlikely to come from the welfare state; yet any solution which ignores the welfare state or tries to dismantle it will fail. A nostalgic return to a coercive, conservative communitarianism will not work in a fluid, individualised society. Too often communities are pockets of prejudice and schools of intolerance. We do not need 'the community' but a country which is rich in communities traditional and technological, religious and secular, sporting and cultural. We will only recreate a sense of 'community' if it is avowedly liberal, voluntaristic, decentralised, self-governing, anti-statist and anti-hierarchical.

To create a modern sense of community we need to open up public spaces where people with diverse interests, skills and resources can meet, debate, listen and co-operate to find common purposes and develop shared values. The private sector is skilled at bringing together a diversity of people as consumers, generally for a commercial purpose. Despite the best efforts of many hard-pressed managers and workers, too often the welfare state seems to divide people rather than bring them together. We will not restore our sense of common purpose as a society unless we reinvent our welfare system.

The trouble is the welfare state was designed for a world which no longer exists. In this country the welfare state, according to William Beveridge, was meant to rid us of want, disease, ignorance, squalor and idleness. There were three main ingredients.

First, a developed system of state social insurance, to protect people against the loss of earnings power: retirement pensions and unemployment benefit; disability and sickness allowances; special tax privileges and benefits for birth and marriage.

Second, the creation of tax financed health and education systems, which nationalised much of the voluntary sector and created a system that was 'free' at the point of delivery.

Third, full-employment policies to put an end to idleness and create the economic basis for a healthy flow of contributions to the social insurance fund and a tax base to finance the new health and education systems.

Five decades later this interlocking system of welfare is collapsing, in large part because the social and economic assumptions on which it was based have fallen apart. Mass joblessness and exclusion have been a feature of our societies for almost two decades. The traditional family has broken up as a dominant model, with the rise of more single and single-parent households. The proportion of elderly in the population is rising fast, beyond the capacity of the traditional social insurance system to keep pace. Technological advances in health care have opened up new demands. The costs of the system are rising as its productivity continues to lag that of the private sector. The quality of many public sector services are often mediocre or worse: they can create a dependency culture among recipients which disempowers them. The public sector is full of well meaning, professional, committed workers and managers, who believe in an ethic of public service. They often work against the odds to provide quality services amidst rounds of cuts and restructuring. Yet despite their efforts the state welfare machine is slow to learn and adapt.

The case for welfare reform seems unsurmountable. Yet it is hugely controversial. Across Europe, in the face of fierce opposition, governments are chipping away at entitlements built up since the war. Virtually everyone is wrapped into the welfare state, as a recipient or contributor. The big budgets of health, social security and education are difficult to keep in check, let alone reduce. Demand-side reform, large scale reductions in entitlements to benefits, are out of the question in this country, at the moment. That means most reform plans focus on the supply-side: making services more efficient through measures such as contracting out and privatisation. Yet even that has met with often understandable scepticism: the internal market in the health service just seems to have created more jobs for managers and administrators. People recognise the severe limitations of the traditional welfare state but fear the consequences of far reaching reform. Most taxpayers do not want to pay more in tax but nor do they support unduly harsh policies against the poor. The safety net may be very badly holed, but it often seems to be all we have. It is widely accepted that we need to move to a new form of social finance – other than tax or traditional social insurance – to mobilise resources for welfare. Yet neither political party has had the courage or imagination to come up with an alternative. So as a society we are stuck.

We shoulder an extremely ineffective and cumbersome welfare state, which is not good at generating a sense of social cohesion, promoting self-reliance or delivering services which match those of the private sector. We know it needs sweeping reform.

Yet we fear losing our own entitlements or being accessories to policies that will punish the poor. We cannot find a way forward.

We need to commit ourselves to a wave of social innovation, lasting years, to create new welfare services and new organisations to deliver them. We need both new ideas and policies, as well as new institutions to deliver them. We need a new generation of welfare institutions which are voluntaristic, open and flexible yet professional, innovative and business-like. To create a new social welfare system we need a new breed of social entrepreneur. Britain has a long history of welfare innovation. At the time of its creation the welfare state was the culmination of this great reforming tradition. Yet one of the greatest costs of the welfare state has been its crowding out of organisations capable of producing welfare reform. We need to return to this voluntaristic tradition of welfare innovation.

Social welfare has never been solely the province of the state. It has always depended on the interaction of three ingredients:

- self-provisioning in the family, with welfare mainly provided by women
- collective and collaborative forms of self-help and mutual assurance through the voluntary sector, friendly societies, trade unions and charities
- state involvement through its regulation of the private sector and direct provision of welfare services.

A new welfare settlement must be based on a new relationship between these three ingredients. As we have seen the welfare state's capacity to meet modern social problems is limited. Families cannot, without more help and support, provide more welfare. Self-provisioning always largely depended on women's unpaid labour: with more women in jobs and more single-parent families, placing yet more of a burden upon over-stretched families is unrealistic. That means the key to a new welfare settlement must come from the second ingredient: new forms of collaborative, mutual assistance provided by organisations which stand between families and the state.

During the hey-day of the welfare state the voluntary sector became the state's junior partner, complementing services provided by the public sector. There was good reason for this. Voluntaristic, charitable welfare provision had not been up to the scale of the social problems created by industrialisation and urbanisation. Diversity of provision brought with it sharp inequalities and unfairness. To many state provision seemed to offer more professional, organised management. Many on the left believed charities and voluntary organisations were antiquated organisations, remnants of an old social order, which provided help motivated by pity and laced with condescension. The left believed the state was the modern solution to social problems: they hoped charities would wither away. Conservatives were much more attached to charities as organic social organisations, which represented long standing traditions of philanthropy and a sense of social order. They too saw charities in a supporting, non-innovative, amateurish relationship with the state.

Yet the centrality of the state in welfare provision is a phenomenon of the latter two-thirds of the 20th century. Before then most of the most important developments in welfare provision have come from the voluntary sector.

One of the greatest periods of social innovation in Britain was in the 12th and 13th century when more than 500 voluntary hospitals were founded. In the 16th and 17th centuries charities and voluntary organisations were one of the few stabilising forces in a society wracked by forces of instability far more powerful than in our own time: epidemics, wars, the enclosures, the growth of a landless poor. It was in this period of then unprecedented social instability that charities came into their own. The growth of philanthropy in the 18th century was superseded in the 19th century by a more clinical, systematic and puritanical approach in the shape of the Poor Laws. Yet the end of the 19th century was probably the hey-day of British charity and philanthropy. Many social organisations were formed by women excluded from business or politics. The labour movement helped to spawn friendly societies, co-operatives, and mutual assurance schemes. By the latter years of the century donations to charity were the second largest single expense in the average middle class household after food.

This vibrant and diverse voluntary sector could not cope, on its own, with the poverty and dislocation of industrialisation and urbanisation. Awareness of the scale of the problems was heightened by the social surveys of Charles Booth and Seebohm Rowntree. Inquiries into the failures of voluntary universities and hospitals highlighted some of the financial and managerial weaknesses of the voluntary sector. The economic dislocation of mass unemployment in the 1930s followed by the sense of solidarity and the scale of state economic organisation during the Second World War, paved the way of the welfare state of Keynes and Beveridge.

Of course we cannot, and should not, turn the clock back to the days before Beveridge when welfare depended on charity. But nor is it true that high standards of welfare can only be provided through the state. On the contrary we need to revitalise and modernise that voluntaristic, non-statist tradition that paved the way for the welfare state. A professionalised, innovative and entrepreneurial sector of social organisations will be a vital ingredient in a modern welfare system.

Social innovation holds the key to our social ills. Social entrepreneurs are the people most able to deliver that innovation.

The value of social entrepreneurs

Social capital and the reform of the welfare state

Even a cursory glance at the projects reported in this study would confirm their quality and creativity. These projects mobilise often discarded resources – a derelict church hall, a hospital about to close, young people who have been written off – to help tackle intractable social problems. They are both entrepreneurial and innovative in spotting and satisfying unmet needs: Mildmay has developed entirely new kinds of services in the field of Aids care; Bromley-by-Bow's partnership with Royal SunAlliance is developing a new way of reducing youth crime, to name just two examples.

Yet despite these achievements two doubts dog the idea that social entrepreneurs could make a lasting contribution to social welfare. These doubts can be summed up as follows:

● These schemes seem good, but is there a systematic way of accounting for the value they create to show that they deliver welfare more effectively?

● These projects are valuable in the particular communities they serve. But could they be extended without robbing them of many of their strengths which stem from their small size and intimate local support?

The answer to the first question is vital to the answer to the second. We need a more systematic way of evaluating these schemes before we can show what role they should play in the future of welfare.

The case for social entrepreneurs rests on the following five pillars.

Problem solving

These schemes help resolve some of the most pressing and intractable social problems our society faces: Aids, mental health, joblessness, illiteracy, crime and drugs.

Social entrepreneurs often confront these problems in new ways and find new solutions. These new approaches could be transferred to the public sector, in much the same way as small biotechnology and software firms often transfer their innovations to larger pharmaceuticals and computer companies. In business we have technology transfer schemes; in welfare we need social innovation transfer schemes. Public policy needs to help to create a much more effective mechanism to identify, interpret and disseminate best practice in welfare provision.

There is a value to society as a whole in promoting a diversity of attempts to tackle problems such as illiteracy or drug dependency. Diversity will help to promote experimentation and expand the portfolio of possible solutions. Of course there are risks to diversity if it leads to unacceptable inequalities and unfairnesses. However at this stage that risk is small compared with the potential benefits from encouraging more experimentation and innovation.

Supply-side efficiency

These projects are often far more cost effective than the welfare state, because they are less bureaucratic, more flexible and capable of generating far greater commitment from their staff.

One example of this is the cost-competitiveness of Kaleidoscope compared with other ways of treating heroin addicts and administering methadone. At

Kaleidoscope the cost is £3.01 per patient, per day, compared with £4 via a pharmacist. It is difficult to obtain comparable costs for the public sector. This operational cost efficiency suggests that society could get far more innovative social welfare, delivered at lower cost, if the welfare state adopted solutions developed by social entrepreneurs.

These skills will become more important as the welfare state is decentralised via contracting out. Already for instance the policy of devolving the local management of schools has required head teachers and school governors to develop more entrepreneurial skills. Decentralisation has further to go: the demand for social entrepreneurship within the public sector will grow.

Public sector trades unions will object that much of the cost-efficiency of non-state organisations comes from their use of non-union, unpaid labour. This objection only goes so far. In many of these organisations staff are highly professional and paid a rate for the job comparable with the private sector. All the organisations profiled in this report would seek to abide by a minimum wage. Much of the higher productivity on these projects comes from greater commitment and flexibility rather than lower pay.

Active welfare

These schemes are developing new models of active welfare, in which users are encouraged to take more responsibility for their lives. In most of these schemes welfare is not seen as a sum of money or even a package of entitlements. Instead most of these schemes embrace a philosophy in which welfare and well-being are inseparable from self-control and self-confidence. These schemes embrace an ethic of creative individualism which is at odds with the passive, recipient culture of much of the traditional welfare state.

These schemes also embody an active ethic of giving, which will become increasingly critical to the traditional welfare state. Hospitals and schools often provide an important focus to bring together divided communities. Yet beyond that the welfare state as a whole is not regarded with much affection. To many of its critics the welfare state breeds passivity, bureaucracy and disillusion.

In contrast social entrepreneurs excel at mobilising a diverse network of people and private sector companies jointly to attack social problems. One prime example of that is the way that Bromley-by-Bow has engaged large companies in the City of London as well as the church and voluntary groups to come up with joint solutions to local problems of crime and youth unemployment.

Jobs and output

Many of these schemes generate benefits which can be measured in traditional economic terms, although many of the entrepreneurs running such projects do not believe this should be an exclusive measure of their success.

Some community enterprise schemes create viable businesses and jobs. In so far as this reduces unemployment and generates valuable output, then this will be of benefit to the economy as a whole, as well as the people involved. Schemes to regenerate housing estates will have measurable benefits in terms of reducing vandalism and crime as well as upgrading the housing stock. Most of these schemes involve upgrading the skills of the people involved to make them more self-reliant. This investment in human capital must have economic value, even if it is difficult to capture in monetary terms.

Perhaps the most important economic argument is hypothetical: what would have happened if these projects had not developed. Had the Mildmay hospital not sprung into life it may well have taken much longer and cost much more for Britain to develop a response for Aids. The investment in various schemes designed to prevent youth crime will pay a return in a reduction in future crime rates and insurance losses.

Social capital creation

Social entrepreneurs create assets for communities which would not otherwise exist. The most obvious examples of these assets are new buildings, new services, or a revived reputation for an area. But in many ways the most important form of capital that a social entrepreneur creates is social capital.

Social capital is the network of relationships that underpins economic partnerships and alliances. These networks depend upon a culture of co-operation, fostered by shared values and trust. The theory of social capital has been developed most effectively by the American social theorist Robert Putnam in *Making democracy work: civic traditions in modern Italy* and by Francis Fukuyama in *Trust*. Both books analyse the role that trust and shared values play in underpinning long term relationships and co-operation, which in turn promote shared efforts at innovation. Social capital matters in the private sector as much as in the voluntary sector. Studies of the success of the German and Japanese economies for instance have underlined the importance of long term relationships and an ethic of co-operation, which provide the basis for their record of innovation and manufacturing prowess.

Social entrepreneurs bring people together in partnerships to address problems which appear insurmountable when they are addressed separately. Social entrepreneurs set in motion a virtuous circle of social capital accumulation. They use networks of support to gain access to buildings and money, to recruit key staff and create an organisation capable of growing. The dividends of this process are rarely financial. The main dividend is itself social: a stronger community, more able to look after itself, with stronger bonds of trust and co-operation.

Conclusions

The value of social entrepreneurs comes in three main forms:

● in the short run, social entrepreneurs may bring measurable benefits to the wider economy by creating jobs, generating output or savings on public spending
● in the medium run, they have great value as potential models for the reform of the welfare state, if they can work more productively in alliance with the public sector
● their more important long run contribution is their ability to create and invest social capital.

The most significant contribution social entrepreneurs make is in helping us to address what is probably the most pressing question our society faces: can a secular society, exposed to the rigours of the global market, based on individual choice, lacking the settled ballast of religion or traditional social hierarchy, in the midst of a global communications explosion also foster a sense of belonging, trust, respect and cohesion? These schemes help us frame some of the answers to this question.

Social entrepreneurs start from a recognition that their environment is complex, fluid and fast moving. They do not retreat into a cosy nostalgia. They embrace that complexity with a determination to be inclusive and compassionate. At their best, these schemes inspire a sense of confidence and optimism, that a modern, mobile society does not have to seem rootless and indifferent.

Social entrepreneurs in action

The stories of five entrepreneurs and their organisations

Introduction

Around the country thousands of social entrepreneurs are at work in organisations which involve tens of thousands of people. Some are little islands within the public sector itself. Most are in what is generally called the voluntary sector. The voluntary sector is vast and amorphous. On its broadest definition the sector is made up of between 378,000 and 400,000 organisations, employing perhaps 950,000 people, about 4 per cent of employment in the entire economy. This sector has an income of perhaps £29.5 billion a year, mainly in culture and recreation, education, health and personal social services. It would be difficult to create a sample representative of the range of innovative and entrepreneurial activity in this sector. That is why we have chosen to concentrate on five case studies, which highlight the strengths and potential of social entrepreneurs as well as the obstacles they face and the dilemmas their work throws up.

The five organisations reported in these case studies are strikingly different. The point of the case studies was to find out whether, despite these differences, social entrepreneurs and their organisations shared important similarities which explained their success. If we can understand what makes social entrepreneurs successful then we stand a better chance of creating more successful schemes. The trials, tribulations, successes and failures of the five entrepreneurs and the organisations which form the core of this report provide a model of social entrepreneurship that could be adopted by policy makers in the public and private sector.

The Bromley-by-Bow Centre

When Andrew Mawson became the United Reformed Church minister in the Bromley-by-Bow area of east London in 1984, he was not over-burdened with resources. His church had a leaking roof, a central heating system that barely worked, a piano with its keys stuck together and an congregation of a few elderly people. It was from this base that Mawson decided to take on the social problems of one of the most depressed neighbourhoods in Britain. Tower Hamlets is the most deprived local authority in the country, according to the Department of the Environment's statistics. The Bromley ward, in which the Bromley-by-Bow Centre sits, wedged between a flyover and acres of high-rise housing estates, is rated the second most deprived ward in the borough. Large private sector employers had virtually deserted the area. Yet despite its deprivation the ward had not received large infusions of public money. It was largely forgotten.

Mawson set about tackling the crisis of the church and the community. He decided the only way forward was to be radical and open. The congregation agreed to offer their under-used buildings to the community, to make of them what they would. The church was redesigned to create a lighter, more open and flexible space that could be both religious and social. These days that space is mainly used as a creche and nursery; it becomes religious at weekends and on some evenings.

The first projects were idiosyncratic. A local woman, a squatter, used the church hall to build a boat. Several local artists moved in to use workshops and provide classes for local people. From that beginning the scheme generated its own momentum. The centre marketed itself through word of mouth, creating an interest that pulled in more people and created more connections. Soon a dance school started, a nursery and a cafe. A disability group started working on the garden outside the church. The dance school eventually became so successful it was floated off as a separate business, located elsewhere. The cafe, which started from a suggestion by a helper at the centre has become a self-sustaining enterprise. The nursery is one of the longest standing projects catering for 30 local children. The disability group evolved into a larger community care programme run on a service contract with the local authority.

More than a decade after Mawson started work the centre is thriving. A £1.4 million health centre, built to the highest standards, housing local general practitioners, is due to be completed soon. The health centre is being built by a development trust, which is run by an executive committee made up of centre users, local councillors and other interested parties. The profits from the centre will go to the development trust to decide how they should be spent. Local people can become members of the trust if they have had a relationship with the Bromley-by-Bow Centre for more than six months. The doctors will rent their workspace from the trust. Mawson says this structure will allow local people much greater say over health priorities because they will be able to determine how any surplus should be spent.

Royal SunAlliance, the insurance group, is funding a £300,000 project over three years to find innovative ways to reduce youth crime in the area. The schedule caters for a core of 50 users, although up to 300 young people have been involved in special events. The scheme is innovative: it runs poetry and sculpture classes as well as foreign trips. It helps local young people gain access to national programmes run by organisations such as the English National Opera. It also runs the only football team in the area to include White, Bengali and West Indian boys.

NatWest Bank has provided a grant of £220,000 to help support local young entrepreneurs. Both these schemes are intended to help young people in the area acquire skills and ambitions which will take them away from drugs and crime. The centre is the base for an outreach project to help provide local Bengali families with literacy skills. The park surrounding the centre is being transformed to create a garden, children's play area and sculpture park. Housing for homeless single young people is being built next door to the centre and plans are afoot to create an enterprise centre, which could serve as a greenhouse for local small businesses.

Mawson and his team have not transformed the area. It still suffers from very high levels of unemployment and deprivation. Yet they have managed to create a centre of excellence and achievement within the community. The centre is the embodiment of some much needed social capital, the basis for the community to shape and respond to its often hostile environment.

At the centre's core is the vision and commitment of a small team of driven, determined people, led by Mawson, and including his deputy Allison Trimble and the finance director Donald Findlay. This full time team created the sense of mission and momentum which has driven the centre's growth. As the centre has grown the management organisation and style has had to develop. Allison Trimble, the centre's chief executive, describes the approach this way:

'It's a loose-tight framework of management. Loose enough to allow people the freedom either to be proactive or to respond quickly to ideas but tight enough to offer a framework of values which contribute to a sense of direction. The key staff are charged with being socially entrepreneurial. They are employed not so much to manage projects but to create environments which will encourage a sense of vision and motivation. We spend a lot of time with project managers when they first start, talking and talking about the values of the centre, telling and re-telling the stories of how it started and grew, until the project managers start creating their own stories themselves.'

The Bromley-by-Bow model is based on five Cs: community members, challenges, creativity, complexity and connections.

Community members
The centre is founded upon a philosophy of openness and inclusion. It starts from its clients and their needs, rather than an imposed idea of what they want. The starting point is not an ideological commitment to one client group or another, but to the community as a whole with all its complexity and confusion. As Allison Trimble puts it:

'The reality of people's lives on these estates is too complex to legislate around ideology or rigid policies, and so, for instance, we do not exclude people from the project for racism or sexism. There is instead a recognition that the language of the street does not always have the abusive meaning interpreted by the politically correct and even when it is abusive the context is generally too complicated to be resolved simply by a policy of exclusion. We have found that excluding people or views simply denies the complexities of the issues.'

The centre aims to move with people as they develop. It does not set arbitrary limits on how far people can go. One example of this was a singing group. They wanted to improve their singing and so asked for help finding a professional teacher. With the teacher providing lessons, they wanted to enter for exams and competitions. Once they had done well in competitions they sang at public events. The group's success at these then brought requests to perform and they started marketing themselves for public functions. At each step of the way the staff at the centre helped the group to move up a ladder of expectations.

Challenges

The centre excels at setting transformatory challenges for its members. Many of the people living close to the centre suffer from a deep-seated lack of self-confidence. The centre aims to lift their sense of self-esteem by proving that they can take on challenges which raise their expectations and confidence.

From the outset Andrew Mawson has insisted on setting high standards. All too often the welfare state has merely helped to entrench a cycle of low expectations, performance and achievement. An ethic of excellence and achievement is at the very heart of the centre; it is a demanding, driven, ambitious place. The buildings are designed and furnished to the very highest standards. The work of artists associated with the project is used to create an imaginative atmosphere. The point is to convince people to think big and aim high. So for instance, the centre's youth project does not provide an echoey hall, with the occasional disco and game of table-tennis. It sends young people on trips across the Sinai desert or for tea at the Ritz.

Creativity

The most important resources the centre possesses are the ideas and knowledge of its staff, helpers and users. Art plays a vital role in this; its influence runs throughout the centre.

Allison Trimble explained: 'We have used the arts to set up environments which encourage contradictions, allow the unexpected to flourish and force people to look again at situations with fresh eyes.'

It is part of the credo of the centre that it should find creative responses to local needs. An example of this is the structure of the health centre. Bromley-by-Bow was determined to create a new way of organising health care that would really involve local people. The result is a centre which is owned by the patients. This creative discipline is one reason why the centre eschews formal mechanisms for community consultation, which are too rigid, slow moving and likely to be dominated by vested interests. The centre prides itself on listening closely and attentively to its community, often seeking out local views. But it does not confuse this with formal mechanisms of consultation.

Complexity
The centre embraces the complexity of the community it serves. More than 80 dialects and languages are spoken within fifteen minutes walk of the centre. A sense of belonging can only be created from such complex ingredients through similarly complicated, overlapping negotiations between users and groups. This embrace of complexity is at the heart of the centre's creativity. If the centre chose to engage with the community in a sentimental, ideological, bureaucratic or compartmentalised way it would not be entrepreneurial and creative, regardless of the drive and imagination of the staff.

The centre is a place where the different currents running through the community can meet and mingle: the secular and the sacred, the public and the private, black and white, young and old. According to Allison Trimble the centre has created a common ground on which people can come together to celebrate their differences. The centre does not seek to brush contradictions and tensions under the carpet for the sake of defending a spurious and sentimental notion of 'the' community. Instead it recognises that the locality is made up of overlapping communities that are sometimes at odds with one another. Rather than pretending this tension does not exist, the centre aims to use it as a source of new ideas. The public sector is part of this picture. Social entrepreneurs regularly bemoan the failings of the public sector. Yet their sense of tension with the public sector is often an important source of their creativity.

Connections

The centre is constantly seeking to make connections between people, institutions and groups who have been kept apart by prejudice, bureaucracy or indifference. The centre's social entrepreneurs are relationship brokers. There are many examples of this search for connections.

One is the way the staff running the community care programme seek to cut across professional boundaries, for instance, between education, health and physical activity to provide an integrated service. Throughout the centre's work, partnerships with the private sector are vital. An example is the youth project which is based on a relationship brokered between an insurance company, Royal SunAlliance, which is concerned about the levels of youth crime and young people, who complain they are attracted to crime because they have nothing to do.

Connectedness underpins the design of the centre's buildings. Spaces are kept open: there are no partitions. They are designed to be used by different groups at the same time, so encouraging people to share and rub shoulders. Allison Trimble explains:

'We have to find ways for the tensions which arise from our diversity to became an opportunity for dialogue and understanding rather than becoming a block to communication. This encourages people to have a sense of ownership about the space and the centre, without that entailing privatisation.'

Connectedness is also at the heart of the centre's style of management. Although there are formal reporting structures and Allison Trimble has regular meetings with her project managers, the management of the centre is open and informal. Trimble spends a lot of time simply wandering around the centre talking. The high level of trust and integration within the centre means that information is readily shared. That means that it is far easier for the senior managers to keep track of what is going on.

The Bromley-by-Bow Centre is a small but inspiring scheme. It combines many of the ingredients of successful social entrepreneurship. At the centre's core are a small team of the founding social entrepreneurs who have imparted the centre's mission and values. This core team, in conjunction with the project managers, have developed a devolved and open style of management which encourages innovation. The form of the organisation has allowed it to engage creatively with a highly complex environment.

Yet the centre's story also highlights some of the many obstacles that social entrepreneurs face. How can small organisations in which the founder plays a vital role manage growth and expansion? As a project expands and grows more complex, how can its sense of mission and purpose be retained? To whom are these social entrepreneurs accountable and how? Can an organisation so heavily dependent on a few individuals organise an orderly succession once the founders are ready to move on? As we will see Bromley-by-Bow is not alone in facing these questions; they are common to all organisations created by social entrepreneurs.

Andrew Mawson

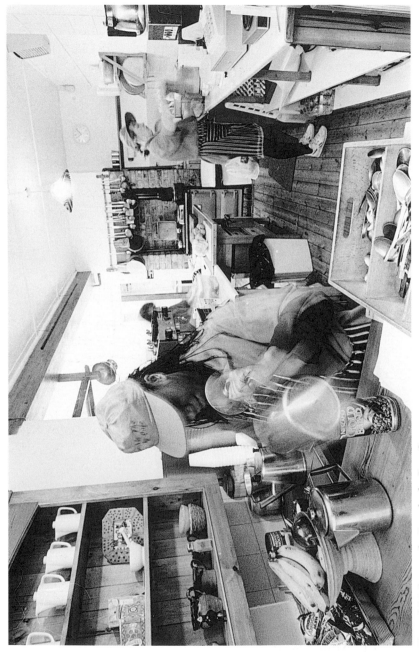

The café kitchen at the Bromley-by-Bow Centre

The Mildmay Mission Hospital

This is the story of how a Victorian hospital which was written off as redundant transformed itself into one of the world's leading centres for Aids care. The district health authority in Tower Hamlets decided in 1982 that Mildmay, an old general hospital on the boundary between Bethnal Green and Shoreditch in London's East End, should close. Helen Taylor-Thompson, who had been involved with the hospital for almost thirty years, was determined it would not shut. She led a tenacious and imaginative campaign to keep the hospital alive. She succeeded. In 1985 one ward re-opened. In 1988 Mildmay admitted its first patients with Aids. In 1997 Mildmay has an international reputation as a centre of excellence for Aids care. It is working in twelve other countries, as well as providing care for single people, parents and children at its Shoreditch base.

All of this has come from a hospital that was abandoned by the public sector as all but worthless a decade ago. The Mildmay's transformation is evidence of how an older charitable tradition of welfare provision – in this case a Christian one – can be drawn upon to create a modern approach to health care, far faster and more effectively than the NHS.

Helen Taylor-Thompson's combative, charismatic, driven personality is central to Mildmay's success. Her mother died when she was a baby. Her father remarried but died on a visit to lay the foundation stone for a hospital in Africa when Helen Taylor-Thompson was nine. Though very close to her stepmother, she says she also grew up with a sense that she would need to fight for her sense of security. Helen Taylor-Thompson was brave and daring: during the Second World War she was involved with special operations forces working behind the lines in France. After the war she went into the family dry cleaning company, where she learned her business skills. She subsequently decided to sell the dry-cleaning business and went into property.

Helen Taylor-Thompson joined the governing council of

the Mildmay about 30 years ago. The hospital was set up by deaconesses from a church in Mildmay Park, Stoke Newington in the 1860s to care for people in Bethnal Green caught by an outbreak of cholera. In 1948 the Mildmay was incorporated into the NHS, as a district general hospital. By the 1980s it was clear that cuts in public expenditure would mean a rationalisation of NHS services into a smaller number of larger hospitals; Mildmay was clearly vulnerable.

The hospital responded by setting up a team to search for a new role. That search brought the hospital into constant battles with the NHS bureaucracy and required a huge investment of voluntary effort, from a close knit group of supporters.

In September 1982 the health authority announced it had decided to close the Mildmay. Many people involved with the Mildmay believed they should accept the inevitability of closure and go gracefully. Helen Taylor-Thompson disagreed. She gathered a group of five people to start a campaign to save it. At that stage the most promising future was to provide beds for local GPs and care for chronically ill, young people.

In February 1983 the health authority said it would investigate whether the Mildmay could become a Christian community hospital, along the lines proposed by the hospital's governing health advisory council. But in July that year the health authority rejected the plan. In November a small group visited Kenneth Clarke, the then health minister, to lobby him to prevent the Mildmay's final closure. They were not successful. In March 1984, he approved the health authority's decision to close the Mildmay. This was probably the lowest point in the hospital's history. A small group of supporters were virtually the only assets the Mildmay had.

Things started to look up in April 1984. The health authority announced a stay of execution, amid hints that the government might approve a plan to turn the Mildmay into a voluntary hospital outside the NHS. After a long campaign to lobby the district and regional health authorities, in which Mrs Taylor-Thompson's contacts in the NHS bureaucracy were vital, the government approved the hospital re-opening as a charity on a 99 year peppercorn rent. The hospital officially re-opened, with very modest ambitions, in October 1985, with its supporters simply glad that they had staved off final closure.

Merely getting to that stage had required the mobilisation of considerable amounts of social capital: the network of the hospital's supporters and Mrs Taylor-Thompson's social and political contacts. But to survive the hospital had to grow, and to grow it had to have a mission that would attract financial support. In reality it had neither. It was a small hospital, with few funds and only a very general idea of what it should be doing. Mrs Taylor-Thompson admits that even then she doubted whether caring for the young chronically sick would provide the hospital with enough of a mission to sustain it. At that stage it was quite possible that the Mildmay could have slowly stagnated and perhaps eventually closed a few years later.

Several factors combined to propel the hospital into a period of rapid, demanding development, which gave it a sense of mission and financial security.

The first was the recruitment of some key staff. Dr Veronica Moss joined the hospital as executive medical director. Several months later Ruth Sims joined as matron. She subsequently became general manager and nursing director before being made chief executive. Dr Moss and Ruth Sims were vital to the hospital's development; they provided an additional injection of skill, motivation, and vision to take it forward.

The second factor was the development of Mildmay's sense of mission. In late 1986 as awareness of Aids was rising, the hospital was approached by a Christian charity, the Care Trust, with a proposal that it should become an Aids hospice. At that time such hospices did not exist; the NHS was yet to develop a distinctive response to Aids.

Mildmay was able to respond far more quickly than the

state. Within a day, Mrs Taylor-Thompson had agreed with Dr Moss and other senior figures at the hospital, that they should take up the Care Trust's proposal. The revised sense of mission had to be negotiated with other supporters, who doubted whether the hospital should become involved in Aids care. The gay community was initially hostile. Yet Mrs Taylor-Thompson's arguments, backed by Dr Moss and Ruth Sims, carried the day. This mixture of decisiveness and flexibility was vital. The initial approach from the Care Trust was made in late 1986. The formal decision that Mildmay should enter the field of Aids care was taken in January 1987.

Mildmay grew by setting in train a circle of development. The initial network of supporters gathered around the hospital was its endowment of social capital. The success of their campaign gave them access to the physical capital of the buildings. The next stage was the attraction of key staff. Together this culminated in the hospital finding a dynamic mission, that could sustain it. The Mildmay was able to embark on a period of rapid development.

The first step was a visit by Mrs Taylor-Thompson, Dr Moss and an architect to San Francisco to learn about developments in Aids care there. One ward of the Mildmay Hospital was converted to care for people with Aids. When this ward took its first patient in February 1988 it was the first Aids hospice ward in Europe.

The new mission brought complications. The hospital was still serving the young chronically sick. The Aids care was attracting a far higher level of financial support. The staff caring for Aids patients were at the cutting edge of their profession. This innovative, entrepreneurial, high-pressure culture was not shared by the staff caring for the young chronically sick.

The hospital governors finally decided that the best way forward for the hospital was to focus on Aids. The care of the young chronically sick, who were consulted about the decision, was taken up by the NHS. This was a difficult but vital decision. Had it not been taken Mildmay would have found it much harder to develop. In almost all organisations growth is only possible if some older aspects of the organisation's work can be left behind. This is vital if managers and staff are to have the time and energy to devote to new opportunities.

The original Aids ward was just the start. Other hospice beds followed. The hospital now has 32 beds for single people. Soon after becoming an all-Aids hospital it opened a day care centre. Ruth Sims quickly became aware of the unmet needs of parents with Aids. A young mother visited the hospital, desperate for care. She had been treated at one NHS hospital which had parted her from her young son. The boy was placed with foster parents, without his mother knowing where he was or who was looking after him. As a result of caring for this mother, Ruth Sims, Veronica Moss and Helen Taylor-Thompson embarked on an ambitious plan to demolish a nurses' hostel and build the world's first purpose built centre to care for families with Aids. The centre has twelve suites where parents can be treated while their children sleep, eat and relax in adjacent rooms, often with other children on the ward. Attached to the centre is a creche where all the children have at least one parent with Aids.

The quality of the Mildmay's work soon started to attract growing interest from abroad. Mildmay will soon open a centre for Aids care and training in Uganda and has provided training and consultancy services in eleven other countries, including Canada, Greece, India, Italy, Japan and Romania. Mildmay's international work is likely to expand.

Even in this most recent period of growth, however, Mildmay has faced serious challenges. The first was financial. By 1989 the hospital had accumulated a large deficit. It managed to pay off this deficit because NHS officials understood how vital Mildmay was in developing a new model for caring for people with Aids. As Mildmay grew it took on more ambitious projects, such as the family centre, which was a strain on its financial and managerial resources.

Just as troubling was the management of Mildmay's mission. Helen Taylor-Thompson's initial aim was to save the hospital. After that the mission was to care for the young chronically sick. That became a mission to care for people with Aids. The adoption of that mission propelled it into a period of growth. The expansion abroad has put further strain on the management and the mission.

Mildmay's involvement with people with Aids in Uganda has forced it to address the social background to the crisis, including the care of children, which some on the council argued lay outside its remit. The expansion overseas proved controversial with some within the hospital who believed it should focus on the UK. Mildmay could not have survived without a mission that allowed it to grow. As it has expanded there has been an ever present risk that the mission might lose focus.

The Mildmay's story highlights many of the obstacles that social entrepreneurs have to overcome.
● It could have developed a mission that would not have sustained it.
● At various times the NHS has been deeply hostile to it.
● It has faced serious financial difficulties.
● The core management team is small, flexible, dynamic and decisive, but it is also very stretched. The Mildmay faces questions about management renewal and succession.

Yet despite these obstacles the hospital thrives. There are several ingredients to the Mildmay's success:
● It is highly entrepreneurial. It has used assets which were virtually written off as worthless to create a world-class hospital.
● It is innovative. It was the first Aids hospice in Europe. It has developed an holistic approach to care by bringing together multi-disciplinary teams of carers, counsellors and medical staff.
● It has combined vision with opportunism and flexibility. When the need for Aids care became apparent it was able to respond far more quickly than the state.

- It has built up a powerful coalition of support, starting with the original, mainly Christian, backers of the Mildmay but extending to draw in other supporters in politics, the gay community and elsewhere.
- The hospital's mission was flexible enough to allow growth and expansion, while providing focus and direction. The mission has neither been too restrictive nor too vague. It has inspired its staff and supporters.

Mildmay is an outstanding success story. Britain has precious few world class institutions: Mildmay is one of them.

A patient relaxing in one of Mildmay's quiet spaces

Helen Taylor-Thompson at the Mildmay Mission Hospital

Kaleidoscope

When Eric Blakebrough arrived at the Baptist Church in Kingston, south London in 1968 he found a congregation of just 25 huddled in a church with a capacity for 600. It was not the most auspicious beginning. The starting point for the Kaleidoscope project was his decision to open a club for young people after the pubs had shut. At the weekend the club stayed open till early on Saturday morning. That brought the minister into contact with a stream of young people with health and drug problems which were not being addressed by the NHS and social services. He decided to start a treatment service as part of the club. From that beginning Eric Blakebrough went on to create one of the most innovative drug treatment programmes in the country.

Kaleidoscope has had a fraught life. It has run into opposition repeatedly from the police and the health service bureaucracy. As recently as two years ago the project was threatened by the decision of a nearby health authority to withdraw funding for 80 of its 300 patients. Kaleidoscope is the most mature of the organisations studied in this report. It exemplifies many of the qualities entrepreneurial social projects need. It also highlights the challenges social organisations face even when they are relatively well established.

In the early 1970s when Eric Blakebrough decided to extend his youth work into drug treatment, NHS drug programmes were rigid and bureaucratic. Detoxification and exacting rehabilitation programmes were virtually the only alternatives to addiction. To gain a place on an official programme an addict had to go through stringent tests, which many of them failed. Frustration with this approach led Eric Blakeborough to devise his own.

He had already persuaded a general practitioner to visit the youth club regularly. In the early 1970s he went a step further and persuaded the Home Office to license Kaleidoscope to provide methadone, a Class A drug, as part of a treatment programme. That has developed into a highly organised programme, in which more than 300 people a day visit the Kaleidoscope building to receive a daily dose of methadone. This daily treatment, which is rigorously administered and checked, is designed to help clients reduce their dependence on heroin and other drugs. Official audits of Kaleidoscope's programme show that it is substantially cheaper than other forms of treatment while being as effective as NHS treatments. The centre has a GP and three nurses, and employs a consultant's services once every two weeks.

After establishing the treatment programme Eric Blakebrough decided Kaleidoscope needed to give young people more structured, long term support. He persuaded five members of the church to re-mortgage their homes to fund a hostel for single homeless young people. Kaleidoscope has a nineteen bed long stay hostel for young people, with a staff of 30 providing counselling, education and training, and supervision. There are art, music and computer workshops as well as job training schemes. The hostel provides young people with a source of stability and permanence; the aim is to help them to become more self-reliant.

Adele Blakebrough, the current director and Eric Blakebrough's daughter, started work at the project twelve years ago. She became director three years ago. Her first task as director was to respond to Merton and Sutton health authority's decision to stop funding places for 80 patients and to take those patients into its own treatment programme. Kaleidoscope kept the patients and the funding but only after a rancorous battle.

Eric Blakebrough managed Kaleidoscope in a personal way. The organisation was highly egalitarian: all staff were paid the same wage. There was no formal management structure to speak of; a wide number of people reported directly to Eric. As the organisation grew this informal approach created its own problems. A personalised management style can appear authoritarian. A lack of formal structures can lead to confusion about roles. Adele Blakebrough put in place a more formal management structure. Line managers were appointed to run different aspects of the centre's work, reporting to her but with considerable day-to-day autonomy. Kaleidoscope policies were codified and written down, rather than being carried by word of mouth. The egalitarian pay structure was replaced with a system which reflected differences in responsibilities and skills

This management reorganisation was vital to provide Kaleidoscope with the opportunity for a new phase of growth. The devolution of responsibility to line managers should allow the director to focus on the next stage of development.

Kaleidoscope has bought the land next to the centre, on which it intends to build an eight bed centre to allow it to deal with Aids patients, plus a purpose built day centre, a restaurant and more workshops to expand the project's vocational training. This next stage of development is still in doubt: Kaleidoscope is embroiled in a legal dispute over planning permission.

Kaleidoscope exhibits many strengths:
● it has been entrepreneurial and innovative, developing a distinctive drug treatment programme which is far more cost effective than similar programmes provided by the NHS
● it has a strong relationship with its clients
● it has successfully managed the transition from management by the founder to a second generation.

Its relations with the state have been complicated and contested. Yet Kaleidoscope is able to innovate because it has identified gaps in the way that official bodies deal with drug dependency. The public sector often finds it difficult to develop integrated, co-ordinated solutions to problems. Kaleidoscope has found it far easier to bring together different skills.

Despite its maturity Kaleidoscope still faces a number of challenges:
● it is controversial in the local community
● its state funding is not completely secure
● it has solved the immediate issue of management

succession, almost as if it were a family business drawing on the new generation: yet this strategy cannot be sustained for ever

● as with many entrepreneurial social organisations it has a complex legal structure involving a church, a commercial arm, a housing association and a charity, all of which require different forms of regulation

● most importantly, Kaleidoscope faces the question of whether it needs to revise and renew its sense of mission to release a burst of growth and provide a new sense of momentum.

Adele Blakebrough

The methadone dispensary at Kaleidoscope

The Youth Charter for Sport

Geoff Thompson often sounds conservative. His philosophy he says is at one with the spirit of the outward bound movement of the 1960s: young people need structure and self-discipline as well as freedom and choice; through physical endeavour they can tap capabilities that lie latent within themselves. Thompson says he is worried by a culture of 'social anarchy' developing among young people. He wants to do something about it.

Thompson, is young, black, charismatic and inspiring. A former world karate champion, he has a simple idea: to use the social capital of his network of contacts with sporting celebrities to create sporting schemes to attract young people away from crime and drugs. The Youth Charter for Sport wants to broker relationships between sporting celebrities and young people, the former attracting corporate sponsorship to schemes to provide young people with a sense of self-discipline.

Geoff Thompson is at the start-up stage of social entrepreneurship. His experience shows how difficult it is to get going even if you have a good idea and contacts. The difficulties he has faced highlight the value there would be in creating a larger, wider network of relationships among social entrepreneurs to share ideas, disseminate best practice and create a jobs market.

Thompson was strongly influenced by the Sport For All philosophy of the Sports Council in the 1970s which helped him to become a karate champion. He wants to reproduce that in the 1990s, but recognises that youth culture has become far less deferential, much more commercialised and far harder to satisfy.

The son of a widow, Thompson says he grew up knowing at least eight father figures. 'We had parents all around us in those days because there were so many more figures of authority that we looked up to,' he says.

In the 1980s when he rose to become a karate champion, Thompson became involved in promoting a wider role for sport. He became a member of the Sports

Council and served on Michael Heseltine's inquiry into the state of inner cities after the riots of the mid-1980s. In the early 1990s, while studying for a business degree at Salford University, he became involved in Manchester's bid for the Olympics. In the course of the bid two drug related shootings of young men in Manchester attracted a great deal of adverse publicity. Thompson decided to respond by organising an event at Wembley in London where 50 children from Manchester and 50 from London joined several sporting celebrities for a festival of sport. At the conclusion all those who took part signed a scroll. That scroll became the basis for the charter.

The next stage of the charter's development came after the Los Angeles riots, when a group of young people from LA came to Manchester. He organised a return visit. The visit helped to transform the outlook of the young people who took part. That led him to set up the Youth Charter for Sport. He has attracted a range of corporate sponsors and partners including Amec, British Airways and Kellogg's. Late in 1996 the Duke of Westminster opened the YCS offices in Salford Quays. Thompson, with a small team of helpers, is hoping to develop the organisation from that base.

Sports celebrities are among the few groups that disaffected young people respect. Partnerships with such celebrities are highly prized by large companies. Sporting celebrities provide a rare bridge between disaffected young people and the world of large corporations. The ethics of sport – co-operation, respect for rules, fair play, excellence – also provide one of the most effective ways of nurturing social values through an activity that young people enjoy. Sport is one of the few meeting places in an increasingly divided society. Thompson believes sporting celebrities should re-invest more in society, especially at a time when large sums of money are being invested in sport through sales of television rights.

It has taken Thompson three years of virtually unpaid work to get YCS to this stage. He has a mission, which is powerfully articulated. What he does not have yet is an organisation or a business. Thompson is at the foot of the development curve. He has an endowment of social capital and some physical capital, but he needs access to financial and organisational capital, human and managerial resources to allow YCS to embark on a period of growth and development. He would like to see YCS offices in most major cities in Britain, promoting sporting links between different groups within society just as the Olympic movement promotes these links between countries.

Geoff Thompson next to graffiti art showing part of the Youth Charter for Sport's philosophy

The computer room at Moss Side Youth Club

The Eldonians

The end of the 1970s was an awful time in Liverpool.
Long-standing working class communities were being
broken up by factory closures and jobs losses as British
manufacturing fell victim to recession and global
competition. The impact of economic decline was
compounded by council plans to re-house people living in
old flats and tenements in peripheral estates and new
towns. The Eldonians began as an act of defiance against
these two forces.

Tony McGann, a charismatic community leader,
organised a group of tenants in estates around Eldon
Street and Burlington Street in Vauxhall, close to the city
centre, to demand better housing. Tony McGann helped to
organise the tenants into the Eldonian Housing Co-
operative. Fifteen years later the organisation McGann
helped to create has built 300 high quality homes on a
crime free estate, which is equipped with a village hall, a
nursery and sports facilities. The Eldonians started as an
act of opposition; it has become the heart of a movement
to regenerate the Vauxhall area as a whole.

At the time the co-operative was created Liverpool City
Council was governed by the then Liberal party. The
Eldonians' development became caught up in the
struggle for power on the council between the Liberals
and Labour and later between different factions within
the Labour party. The Liberal council, keen to make in-
roads in staunchly Labour wards, helped to promote the
co-operative. It was not just power politics. The Liberals
had a history of support for community action. The
Eldonians' first project was the Portland Gardens housing
scheme, a co-operative development of 130 homes on five
vacant sites. Tenement blocks were refurbished into two-
story houses and sheltered housing units.

The success was to be short lived. In 1983 the Militant
faction within the Labour party took control of the
council and the co-operative was municipalised. Despite
this takeover Tony McGann and others managed to keep
the Eldonians alive as a social network.

When Militant was toppled in the late 1980s, the social capital underlying the Eldonian project – its network of supports and contacts – was still in place. The community spirit was sustained largely through the Community Trust, which ran welfare services for old people. It established a Community Development Trust, with the aim of creating small businesses in the area.

With the closure of the Tate & Lyle sugar refinery the Eldonians were given the go-ahead to reform the Housing Co-operative and to use the vacant site to build homes. The first phase of the Eldonian village was completed eight years ago: 145 homes, built to the highest standards, with the tenants intimately involved in the design of their houses. The village has been set out with the involvement of crime prevention officers: as yet there has not been a single burglary on the estate. The Eldonians describe it as a crime free environment.

After the completion of the first phase, the co-operative turned itself into a community based housing association. The association took on the second phase, with the help of the Merseyside Development Corporation and the Housing Corporation, to build a further 150 homes. In all, the village accommodates 310 homes, including fifteen sheltered housing units.

A third phase of housing is planned for an adjacent site, further along the Leeds and Liverpool canal, which cuts through the village. This will include homes for rent, and shared ownership schemes, in which people will be invited to buy their own homes in partnership with the housing association. Tony McGann and the small, over-stretched team that helps him, insist that from the outset the Eldonians were more than a housing scheme: they have a larger ideal of community sustainability.

The village includes a village hall, which is the focus for community events, and sports facilities. A recently opened bowling green and five-a-side football pitch will soon be joined soon by an indoor health and fitness centre. A nursery provides fee-paying places for people on the estate as well as employees of Littlewoods.

The Eldonians' work is increasingly focused on enterprise creation and training. The overwhelming majority of the population of the estate are without work. The Community Development Trust is working with local businesses and companies that might invest in the area to develop training schemes to promote employment. It has also created a number of community businesses, although these are inevitably small and their growth is limited by the lack of spending power in an area beset by high unemployment. With Liverpool council's economic development unit, the Eldonians are developing plans to create an information technology centre. The organisation is planning to collaborate with other voluntary organisations in the area to regenerate the area as a whole. Several voluntary organisations are working on a plan to create a local credit union, for instance.

The Eldonians is a hugely impressive scheme:
- it has provided high-quality housing for local people
- it has created a social infrastructure of sporting and social facilities
- it is helping to provide education and training opportunities in an area desperately short of work
- most importantly it has helped a community to stand together and created the basis for its efforts at renewal and regeneration.

At the heart of the organisation is a charismatic, visionary entrepreneur, Tony McGann, who has injected a constant flow of energy into the project, in part through his ability to build political and social alliances in a sectarian city. McGann has helped to build a small, flexible organisation, which is committed to innovation and development. Most importantly from the outset it has always engaged with its clients as members.

The sense of ownership and pride people feel in the Eldonian village stems directly from the way that they were involved in the design of their houses. It was written into the project from the start that old and young people, single people and couples, families and people without children, would have different needs. A precondition of their coming together in a joint sense of ownership of the village is that their distinct needs should be recognised. Had the complexity and diversity of their needs been overridden by a rigid plan, then the basis for their involvement would have been undercut; the possibility of their creating a community would have been denied.

Another vital ingredient in the Eldonians' success has been its insistence on the highest possible standards. The houses are thoughtfully designed, well built and professionally maintained. By instilling the highest possible standards in the physical environment, the project has created expectations among its members of high quality treatment in other aspects of their lives.

Three other aspects of the Eldonian project stand out. First, the centrality of the scheme's complex relationship with the state. The state has not been an enduring and predictable factor in local development. It has been changeable and disruptive. Power has swung between parties and ideologies within parties. The state has taken different forms including Liverpool council, the Merseyside Development Corporation, a string of government departments and latterly the European Commission. Social entrepreneurs do not deal with a single state; they deal with many different parts of the state.

This cuts both ways. Change can be disruptive: the switch from Liberal to Labour control of Liverpool council almost killed off the Eldonian project before it got started. The multiple forms the state takes makes life cumbersome and time-consuming. However an overly close, clientelistic relationship with the state could rob social entrepreneurs of their independence and innovation. Social entrepreneurs thrive amidst the failures of the state.

Second, the Eldonians, in common with many similar organisations, have been forced by charity and commercial law to develop an overly complicated legal structure. The Eldonian project encompasses a community trust and a community development trust, which have created a number of community businesses and a housing association. Each is regulated and governed in a slightly different way. Life would be a lot easier for entrepreneurial social organisations if there was a single, hybrid legal structure which encompassed their commercial and charity work.

Third, projects such as the Eldonians are particularly vulnerable to the changeable character of the state because other partners and funders are so difficult to find in such a rundown area. There are few large local businesses that could serve as private sector partners. Projects such as the Eldonians need access to a wider network of private sector partners.

Anyone who sets foot in the Eldonian village would be impressed. Amid economic decline, political turmoil and social upheaval it has managed to create a sense of community by understanding the diversity of its members' needs, building alliances and delivering high standards of service. It is difficult to imagine a better model of community regeneration.

Tony McGann at the Eldonian Village development

Pupils at the nursery in Eldonian Village

Case studies: conclusions

Policy makers are increasingly attracted to the voluntary sector because it is widely assumed voluntary organisations are flexible, responsive, innovative and cost-effective. That is far from true of the sector as a whole. Much of the voluntary sector is slow moving, amateurish, under-resourced and relatively closed to new ideas. However these case studies have highlighted a number of vital ingredients which promote innovation:

(i) At the heart of all these projects stands a dynamic social entrepreneur, who drives the project on. Without this central figure none of these projects would have got started. However the mere presence of a social entrepreneur will not be enough to create an entrepreneurial social organisation.

(ii) One of the main tasks of the founder in all these case studies has been to create a wider organisation, which is flexible, flat, with a strong culture of creativity and openness. However, even that is not enough to explain why these organisations are entrepreneurial. Plenty of voluntary organisations have strong leaders and flexible organisations without being innovative. A third factor is involved.

(iii) All these organisations adopt a complex, open and dynamic relationship with their users, partners and funders. These organisations have generally started with a specific aim but then developed wider ambitions. They do not think of providing clients with a set product or service but rather as building a relationship that develops over time. This means the organisation has to be open to change.

All these organisations operate in complex environments, where several state agencies might be addressing the same issue in separate ways. This creates opportunities for social entrepreneurs to bridge gaps between different agencies and broker multi-disciplinary approaches. Successful social entrepreneurs build wider networks, through which they get ideas, people and money. The wider the network, the greater diversity in the new ideas the organisation is likely to get.

A voluntary organisation could be run by a visionary, inspiring leader and have a flat, non-hierarchical structure, but fail to innovate if its relationship with its clients is closed and consumerist, or if it deals with a specific arm of the state and has only a few external partners.

(iv) Successful social entrepreneurs create a cycle of development that goes through several stages. Social entrepreneurs start with an endowment of social capital in the form of a network of contacts and supporters. This gives them access to physical and financial capital which they can use to develop the organisation. The next step is the recruitment of further key people (human capital) and the development of a wider organisation (organisational capital) to allow the organisation to expand. If this phase is successful the organisation can enjoy strong growth with the creation of a string of new products and services as well as an infrastructure of buildings. This infrastructure becomes the social dividend of the process and the basis for a further phase of investment.

The social entrepreneur creates this circle of social capital accumulation. At each stage of this circle social entrepreneurs need different kinds of support to reach the next step.

(v) These organisations are not static; it is in their character to grow. Growth makes it easier to attract and motivate users, staff and partners. This drive to grow is vital, but as the organisation grows it becomes more complex, more difficult to manage and more vulnerable financially. Understanding the phases of growth that these organisations go through will be vital to designing policies to support them.

These five ingredients make up our model to explain successful social entrepreneurship:

- the social entrepreneur
- the nature of the organisation they create
- the organisation's interaction with its complex environment

- the circle of social capital accumulation the social entrepreneur sets in train
- the lifecycle of the organisation which takes it from inception, through growth to maturity.

With this model it is possible to explain what makes social entrepreneurs successful, how we might foster more of them and how more of them can be encouraged to grow their organisations to maturity. We briefly examine each element of this model in turn.

Who are social entrepreneurs?

The qualities, skills and values it takes to be a social entrepreneur

At the heart of the organisations profiled in this report stands a social entrepreneur who drives the organisation. None of these organisations could exist without the leadership of the charismatic individuals at their heart. Social entrepreneurs will be a vital source of the wave of social innovation Britain needs to confront the new challenges faced by the welfare state. But what makes a social entrepreneur? Social entrepreneurs are:

entrepreneurial: they take under-utilised, discarded resources and spot ways of using them to satisfy unmet needs

innovative: they create new services and products, new ways of dealing with problems, often by bringing together approaches which have traditionally been kept separate

transformatory: they transform the institutions they are in charge of, taking moribund organisations and turning them into dynamic creative ones. Most importantly they can transform the neighbourhoods and communities they serve by opening up possibilities for self-development.

Successful social entrepreneurs all have the following qualities. They are: leaders, storytellers, people managers, visionary opportunists and alliance builders.

Leadership

The quality that all social entrepreneurs have in abundance is leadership. They are very good at setting a mission for an organisation and mobilising people around it.

A sense of mission is vital for all non-profit organisations because it provides them with their sense of purpose. In most companies financial or commercial measures, such as shareholder value, profitability or market share provide a sense of purpose and direction. In voluntary organisations this guiding purpose is set by its sense of mission.

The mission is the flag around which staff, users and supporters can gather even when there is little to show by way of services or physical infrastructure. Creating a sense of mission involves several steps. The mission has to connect with the unmet needs of a group of users. It cannot be too abstract or vague. It should be challenging and demanding. Successful social entrepreneurs set an ambitious mission which helps them to transform the organisation and achieve much more than they thought was first possible. Successful business leaders frequently do this: they set their companies very ambitious targets – dramatic improvements in productivity and quality for instance – to encourage staff to think radically.

The mission has to be coherent and clear enough to command support, but flexible enough to allow growth. These organisations need to grow to generate the support and enthusiasm which keeps them going. Social entrepreneurs have to be good at 'mission management' as well as 'mission setting'.

Storytelling

Social entrepreneurs have to be good at communicating the mission. Successful social entrepreneurs are good storytellers.

This storytelling capacity marks them out from business executives and politicians. Ask executives to explains their businesses and they will most likely talk analytically about market share and product segments. Ask politicians what they stand for and they will treat you to a mixture of abstract values, detailed policies and well-honed sound bites. Ask social entrepreneurs and they will most likely tell you a story about how a person transformed their outlook by being involved with the project.

Social entrepreneurs communicate their values and motives through stories and parables. This is what makes social entrepreneurs so compelling and persuasive. It encourages other staff and users to think imaginatively rather than analytically or procedurally.

People

These organisations are people businesses par excellence: they usually have no other resources. Social entrepreneurs recognise that the knowledge and ideas of their staff, helpers and users are their most important resources.

They have to be very good with staff, especially in recruiting the key staff at the early stage of a project who can help to carry it forward. Social entrepreneurs deal in people and opportunities rather than plans and procedures.

Visionary opportunists

Social entrepreneurs are visionary: they communicate their aims in moral terms. But they do not get hung up on plans and strategies. They are pragmatic and opportunistic. If an opportunity comes along they will try to take it, even if it does not fit their original plan. Social entrepreneurs are visionary, but they are not sentimental, especially about their clients. They are realistic about the nature of the problems their users confront. These projects see their users as active and demanding people rather than dependent, passive recipients of welfare services.

Alliance building

Social entrepreneurs are alliance builders. Their organisations are usually too poor and too frail to survive on their own resources. They can only survive by depending upon a wider network of support. Social entrepreneurs will only succeed if they are good at establishing these networks of support. Successful social entrepreneurs are all good at networking. They will talk to anyone, of any political persuasion, if they think the conversation might help their project.

They are ideological chameleons: they cannot be tied down to a political position as this would cut them off from potential supporters.

They do not accept a single, simplistic explanation for the problems they deal with. Social entrepreneurs, driven by the need to address real problems, have already gone beyond the traditional divisions of left and right, market and state.

Their language is caring, compassionate and moral. Yet that does not mean they identify with the liberal left: they are highly critical of the statism of the old left and sentimentalised versions of working class communities. They recognise that economic dislocation and global competition have contributed to many of the social problems they are dealing with. But that does not make them anti-business. Instead they recognise the importance of benchmarking the standards of their own services against those of the private sector.

They would completely reject the libertarian right's radical individualism. Yet they accept much of the right's critique of the way the welfare state has created a dependency culture among many benefit recipients.

This ideological flexibility and intellectual agility underpins their ability to innovate.

Questions and doubts

Social entrepreneurs create thriving organisations out of virtually nothing. They need great strengths, particularly leadership skills. Yet these very strengths also create difficulties for people who deal with them. It is important to understand the nature of these difficulties because they represent real constraints on the expansion of social entrepreneurship.

Accountability

Social entrepreneurs hate committees and bureaucracy. They find the procedures the state uses to account for public money cumbersome and tiresome. This raises doubts in the minds of civil servants and local authority officials about whether social entrepreneurs are willing to be held accountable for the way they spend public money. This is part of a larger question which is often answered only vaguely by social entrepreneurs themselves: to whom are they accountable?

Entrepreneurs in all walks of life do not like being constrained by boards or committees. They often run highly personalised businesses without formalised procedures and processes.

Social entrepreneurs would say in their defence that they are accountable to their clients through the quality of the services they run. They tend to run open organisations in which staff and users are encouraged to voice their views. Formal committees often give power to people skilled at running committees. There is a serious issue here, which many social entrepreneurs have not addressed adequately. It may be that through the developing contract culture in the public sector a more negotiated form of accountability can be established through dialogue with public sector funders about the aims and performance of schemes.

Before social entrepreneurs claim to be ready to run a large part of welfare provision they will have to show there are mechanisms to ensure they are publicly accountable. That accountability needs to come in a form that does not compromise the very qualities for which they are prized: their independence and innovation. Voluntary organisations and independent parts of the public sector, such as opted out schools, would find it useful to experiment with different forms of accountability and user involvement, including citizens' juries, forms of plebiscite and other forms of consultation.

Missing skills

Social entrepreneurs often lack important skills that will be particularly valuable as their organisations get larger. They often need to develop executive and analytical skills to help them manage larger, more complex organisations, which have larger financial commitments.

Succession

Small businesses often find it difficult to bring on a second generation of entrepreneurs to run a business once the founder has retired. Social entrepreneurs need to think carefully about managing the succession to a new generation of managers. In large businesses that job is usually done by members of the board. There is an executive recruitment market to turn to, a host of people running similar businesses as well as internal candidates. In the commercial world small businesses often sell themselves to larger businesses when the founder decides to retire.

With social entrepreneurs the task of organising an orderly succession is more difficult. There is no external job market. The boards of these organisations are rarely organised well enough to take on the task. In the world of social entrepreneurs there is no market in which to sell a business. These organisations will only be long lasting if they have a orderly way of ensuring management succession. As yet most do not have such a mechanism.

Scale

Even if these organisations were given large sums of money to run welfare programmes they probably would not cope because they do not have enough managerial depth.

At the moment they are small and medium sized businesses which do not seem capable of becoming national or international businesses, with franchised operations and subsidiaries around the country. Mildmay comes closest to this model. It is on the verge of quasi-franchising its approach to Aids care internationally. But as yet most social entrepreneurs lack the resources and skills to achieve such an extension of their activities.

This raises questions about the appropriate aims of public policy. It may be some time before individual organisations emerge which are robust enough to take responsibility for delivering large chunks of publicly funded social welfare programmes. A more realistic goal would be to create a larger population of small scale social entrepreneurs.

A policy of 'picking winners' by trying to guess the most likely sources of social entrepreneurs is probably pointless. People cannot be taught to become social entrepreneurs. What can be taught are some of the skills social entrepreneurs need to help them to survive.

Conclusions

The social entrepreneurs profiled in this report are all impressive people. They have achieved a great deal with limited resources. A voluntary organisation cannot be entrepreneurial without a social entrepreneur at its heart. However the presence of a social entrepreneur is not enough to guarantee that an organisation will become entrepreneurial and innovative. For that to happen further ingredients are needed. In particular we need to look at the kinds of organisations that social entrepreneurs create and the way that they interact with their users, partners and funders.

Flat and flexible

How redundant organisations become dynamic and innovative

Social entrepreneurs are most effective when they create entrepreneurial organisations, which interact with their environment in an innovative way. That is when they start creating new forms of welfare service. The link between the social entrepreneur, the organisation and their environment is vital. This chapter examines the main characteristics of these organisations.

Structure

Entrepreneurial organisations tend to have flat management structures, with virtually no bureaucracy. At their most complex the director or social entrepreneur works with a small team of senior staff and a group of line managers who are responsible for specific projects. Lines of communication are short. Formal reporting structures are less important than informal consultation and discussion. Access to the senior staff is very open, and decisions are often taken speedily.

Full time staff

Entrepreneurial social organisations usually start with at least one full time staff member, however poorly paid. A full time staff, however small, is vital. Innovation is much more difficult if the staff is a shifting army of volunteers and secondees.

Culture

Entrepreneurial organisations develop a culture of creativity. They set out to respond to needs in an innovative way. Successful entrepreneurial social organisations set themselves high standards to aim at, which force them to think imaginatively.

Creativity most usually comes about when people are working together, often in small groups, sharing ideas. This works best when people trust one another. The organisations profiled in this report generate large reservoirs of trust.

Governance

As there are no shareholders to report to, the role of the board is often uncertain, other than being the trustees of the charitable arm of an organisation. It is not clear to whom the board is accountable or for what. These organisations need relatively small, committed and creative boards. Yet often they are required by law to include several different bodies – a charity, a commercial arm and a housing association – each with its own board. As a result it is often difficult for one board to take a view of the entire project. An effective board, especially with an effective chair, can play a vital role in helping to develop a project.

Conclusions

Entrepreneurial social organisations have flat, devolved management structures. They rely on a small band of full time staff and employ informal management styles. However this combination does not explain why these organisations are innovative. Many voluntary organisations have flat, non-hierarchical management structures. And yet most are not innovative or entrepreneurial. A third ingredient is at work in innovative organisation: how they interact with their environment.

Thriving on complexity

How social entrepreneurs embrace change

Social organisations are more likely to be entrepreneurial and innovative if they interact with their environment in two ways:

- they operate in a relatively complex and fluid environment, in which new demands and opportunities open up.
- they develop an evolving relationship with their clients which gradually opens up more complex needs and demands.

Voluntary organisations can be localised, particularistic and inward looking, dealing with a narrowly defined client group and a fixed idea of their users' needs. Organisations of this kind are rarely innovative. That does not mean that the work they do is not valuable. On the contrary voluntary organisations, particularly self-help groups, often address specialist and particular needs that the welfare state is unable to satisfy.

However the focus of this report is on the kind of innovation we need to generate more effective approaches to welfare. The organisations profiled in this report have become innovative because they adopt an open and complex relationship with their environment.

Users

Entrepreneurial social organisations, like the best businesses, recognise they are dealing with users who have complex needs. They do not think of themselves as providing a specific service or product. Instead they see their job as satisfying the needs of their clients and using a range of different services to achieve that end.

Kaleidoscope for instance does not simply regard its job as providing methadone maintenance; its job is to work with its clients' varying needs which might require medical treatment, psychiatric care, counselling, education, art therapy and so on. If Kaleidoscope understood its job as simply doling out methadone it would be virtually indistinguishable from a large pharmacy.

Funders

Entrepreneurial organisations often have a complex and creative relationship with their funders, rather than a simple, contracted out one. The funders often go to the organisation to help find creative solutions, rather than a specific service.

They usually rely upon both public and private sector finance. Their relationship with the state is often complicated.

Often the problems these organisations are dealing with – crime, joblessness, health, drugs – are being addressed by several local and national state agencies at the same time. It is also common for several groups of professionals to be involved – teachers, the police, doctors, psychiatrists, social workers – each with their own agenda and priorities.

This separation of agencies and professions often means the state misses opportunities to find creative solutions. Social entrepreneurs thrive on these missed opportunities. Social entrepreneurs stand outside the rigid demarcation lines of the state and the professions. This allows them to spot innovative ways of combining resources and people that are traditionally kept in their separate pigeon holes.

Simple, stable environments create few incentives for creativity. Innovation thrives amid complexity and change.

Partners

In the private sector, market economy competition is the greatest spur to innovation. Companies innovate to gain a competitive advantage. They often achieve this by working co-operatively with their suppliers and product development partners. Co-operation is playing a growing role in corporate life, but competition is still the driving force.

In the voluntary sector competition is becoming more important than it was, as organisations compete for funding. Yet co-operation is far more likely to be the source of innovative ideas and the means of seeing them through. Managers in entrepreneurial social organisations have to be good at managing co-operation.

The most effective substitute for the market is a wide network of partners and contacts, who bring new ideas, resources, people and opportunities to the organisation.

The wider and more diverse the network of partners and supporters, the richer the flow of different ideas and opportunities. The more isolated and atomised the organisation, the less likely it is to be innovative. The characteristics of innovative and non-innovative organisations are set out in Figure 2 (opposite).

Conclusions

Voluntary organisations are entrepreneurial and innovative when they combine:
● a dynamic, social entrepreneur to lead the organisation
● a flat, open management structure with a culture of trust and creativity
● a complex, changing environment, which the organisation embraces.

Figure 2. Social organisations

	INNOVATE	STAGNATE
ENVIRONMENT	Complex Multi-agency	Simple Clientelistic
CLIENTS	Evolving	Specific
FUNDS	Some security	Precarious
EXTERNAL LINKS	Networked Many	Isolated Few
MISSION	Expansive Encourages growth	Narrow Limits growth
STAFF	Core full-time	Volunteers
LEADERSHIP	Inspirational Driven Outward looking	Cautious Servicing Inward looking
CULTURE	Open Creative Other regarding	Closed Conservative Self-regarding

This set of relationships is set out in Figure 3 opposite. If an organisation is successful its interaction with its environment becomes part of the organisation's character. The best entrepreneurial social organisations are organic and evolutionary, they develop with their users and partners. They are porous at the edges; the boundary between the organisation and its users is not fixed.

Charles Handy, the management thinker, distinguishes two types of voluntary organisation: 'self-regarding' organisations, which mainly provide services for their members (The Women's Institute for instance), and 'other regarding' organisations, which serve strangers and provide hardly any services for members (Oxfam). Entrepreneurial social organisations break through this distinction. They usually exhibit a strong sense of membership and association, because users identify very strongly with the organisation. Yet they are not run for the members. They are not closed and inward looking.

This raises an important point about the structure of these organisations. They are often forced by the law to adopt unnecessarily cumbersome and complex structures, usually involving a charity, a trading arm and often a housing association and a church. Some of these forms allow for membership and even share-ownership, while others do not. Many organisations find themselves squeezed into legal strait jackets which are designed for other organisations. The requirements of the government and the charity commissioners often wrap these organisations in unwarranted red tape. Entrepreneurial social organisations would be helped immensely if there was a more flexible, off-the-shelf, legal form they could adopt, to provide a single structure to cover both their charitable and trading activities, which could allow some form of membership. Such legal structures exist elsewhere in Europe but not yet in the UK.

Figure 3. The social entrepreneurial organisation

THE ENVIRONMENT

THE ORGANISATION

THE SOCIAL ENTREPRENEUR LEADERSHIP MISSION SETTING

Flat
Flexible
Open
Creative

Complex
Changing

Boundary between organisation & environment porous

THE ORGANISATION

THE ENVIRONMENT

The virtuous circle of social capital

How social entrepreneurs inherit, create and invest social capital

Successful social entrepreneurs go through a cycle of growth in several linked stages. At each of stage they could fail and the organisation could go into decline. At each stage they need different skills and support, from their partners and funders. Understanding the steps in this cycle is essential to understanding how successful social organisations develop.

There are six steps to the development of entrepreneurial social organisations, set out in Figure 4 (opposite). We call this process the 'virtuous circle of social capital' because it starts with the inheritance of social capital and its ends with the returns from the investment of social capital.

1. Endowment
All social entrepreneurs start with an endowment of social capital: a network of relationships and contacts, which are tied together by shared values and interests.

Social capital is vital to social entrepreneurs: they usually have little else to start with.

The first job of the social entrepreneur is to take whatever endowment of social capital he is given and to use these relationships to create more social capital, by

Figure 4. The virtuous circle of social capital

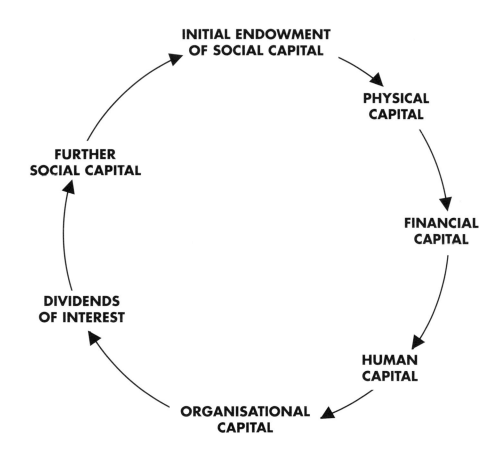

getting more people and organisations involved with the project, by building a wider web of trust and co-operation around the project. With this start-up fund of social capital the social entrepreneur can then get access to the physical, financial and human capital needed to get the show on the road.

2. Physical capital

The initial endowment of social capital often brings access to physical capital, usually in the form of rather run down buildings. Getting access to a physical base is vital. It provides a focus, a base for new services and a tangible sign that the project is achieving something.

3. Financial capital

A lot of goodwill and a run-down building can only get you so far. In addition social entrepreneurs need some start-up funds, though often not that much.

The initial network of supporters and helpers is vital to bring access to funds, through fundraising, donations and corporate giving. The more diverse and richer the network, the easier it will be to raise the funds.

4. Human capital

Armed with social, physical and financial capital, it is only possible for the project to get started if it recruits the right people. If at this stage only the founding social entrepreneur is involved the project will run into a bottleneck: it will not have enough of the right people to put the capital to work effectively. So the project has to recruit and pull in more key people to help it move from start-up into growth, creating products and services.

5. Organisational capital

At this point the project should start growing rapidly, pulling together all the capital invested in it – social, physical, financial and human – to generate a range of new products and services. This is the most exciting and uplifting phase of any project. As these services are launched, new users and partners are drawn into the project, new ideas are developed and new relationships formed. As the project grows, becomes larger and more complex, its management will need to become more organised. It will need stronger financial systems and legal help. With more staff involved, people management may become more complicated. With a wider mix of products and services, there will be difficult questions about whether new services should take priority over existing ones.

In this period the project needs to develop organisational capital: a more formalised management structure, financial systems, a stronger set of relationships with partners.

6. Paying dividends

In the first phase of the project the social entrepreneur inherits and creates social capital. Then he starts to accumulate more capital in the form of buildings and finance. Then the capital is invested in creating new services and products. In the final phase, if the investment has been successful the project starts to pay dividends in several different forms. One may be the creation of a permanent, physical infrastructure, with assets that are of great value to the community – a revived community centre, a re-opened hospital, sporting facilities. Perhaps the most valuable dividend is yet more social capital, in the form of stronger bonds of trust and co-operation, within the community and with outside partners and funders. This wider network of relationships can become the basis for a further stage of development. The dividends become the endowment for a new cycle of investment and development.

The main task of the social entrepreneur is to set this cycle in motion. An organisation is successful when it manages to get this circle moving very fast, pulling in new partners and users to create a flow of new products and services. The organisation also has to be able to slow down if it needs to consolidate. If the circle grinds to a halt the organisation will go into decline: it will start eating up its fund of goodwill and trust without replenishing it.

It is illuminating to compare the activities of social entrepreneurs with those of the welfare state and the private sector. The welfare state is blessed with a lot of physical and financial capital. Yet it destroys social and human capital as often as it creates it. It is too bureaucratic to generate the relationships of trust and goodwill, which can start to revive a sense of community and solidarity.

The private sector relies on social capital, but it all too rarely creates it. Private sector companies depend upon a relationship of trust with their employees, consumers and the communities where they operate. Yet all too often restructuring, delayering and downsizing have destroyed these bonds of social capital.

The life cycl of social entre- preneurship

How social entrepreneurs inherit, create and invest social capital

Growth is the lifeblood of these organisations. Yet once an organisation starts to grow it creates strains and pressures which create unforeseen problems. Social entrepreneurs are restless. They do not like to sit back and admire their good work. Yet it is not just these psychological qualities which drive their organisations to grow. Growth is essential because it satisfies organisational imperatives. These organisations are built upon the energy and enthusiasm of people. To attract these people and motivate them, they need to be given new challenges, new opportunities. Money and fame are not available as motivators. The only really motive force is the excitement and pleasure of achievement. To provide a stream of new opportunities an organisation has constantly to develop and grow.

Yet growth brings a range of difficult problems. The life cycle of growth that entrepreneurial social organisations go through is set out in Figure 5 (overleaf). We examine in turn the strains of growth these organisations face and how they resolve them.

Figure 5. The life cycle of the social entrepreneur

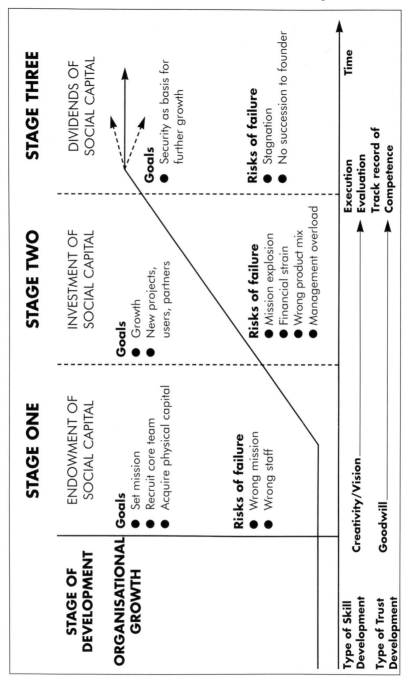

Mission management

The mission sets an organisation's purpose and its
boundaries by determining the activities it will invest in.
But as an organisation develops, troubling questions are
raised about what activities lie within the boundaries of
the mission and what lie beyond its scope. The questions
raised within the Mildmay about the extent of its
international work are an obvious example of this. The
organisation must have a creative approach to revising its
mission. It must find time to think and imagine what it
might become. This is always quite difficult in busy,
financially stretched organisations. The management
team must find a way of getting all those involved with
the project to buy into the revised sense of mission. This
process is fraught with risk. If the procedure is too formal
it can become cumbersome without engaging people. If
the management team does not consult enough it may
find it does not have the support of some key
constituencies.

Another risk is that the mission can be captured by one
group within the organisation which will impose its own
agenda. For instance in most financially stretched
organisations there is a constant threat that the mission
may be captured by the funders, who set conditions on
funding which determine what the organisation can do. A
different risk is that the consumers dominate the
organisation too much and effectively set prices for
services so low that the organisation runs into financial
problems.

Product mix

Entrepreneurial social organisations grow because they
respond to emerging client needs. That means they are
often being asked to provide new services.

Yet developing a wider range of services carries risks.
As new services develop they often displace existing ones.
More management time and effort will be devoted to the
new service at the expense of the existing activities. In
some cases it may be essential for an organisation to

jettison or de-merge some of its original activities to allow growth.

The development of commercial activities creates particular problems. Money making ventures often involve greater financial risk than other projects. The demand that they make money creates a measure of their success that can distract attention from other schemes which are harder to evaluate. As a result small commercial activities can take up a disproportionate amount of management time. Judging what is core to an organisation is always very difficult. The best product extensions are those that build upon an organisation's core skills and competencies. Yet deciding what those core skills are is often more difficult than it first appears.

Governance

As an organisation grows its governance often becomes more complex. There are more funders, partners, clients and staff. In addition it is quite likely that an single organisation will have to develop several arms, each with their own legal, tax and governance structure. This often makes for complicated decision making and cross-cutting lines of accountability.

Analysis and evaluation

Organisations need to acquire a range of new skills as they develop. At the outset there is a high premium on creative qualities as the entrepreneur defines the mission and gathers the capital needed to get going. During this early phase the organisation generates and depends upon a great deal of goodwill among its partners who identify with the project's aims.

As the project gets larger and more complex, the management needs to acquire executive and analytical skills as well as creative ones. As a scheme takes on contracts to develop services it needs to get better at executing and delivering what it has promised to undertake. The organisation needs to build a reputation based on its track record.

Once an organisation becomes more mature, with a portfolio of schemes and services under its wing, it is particularly important that it should become better at evaluating its work. It needs to become better at evaluation for several reasons:

● to make the case to its donors, clients and the public at large that the organisation is effective and useful in its spending

● to allow the organisation to re-align its organisation and management to meet goals set by the mission which are not being met

● to guide its investment decisions and make the case to potential funders that it should be given more money.

Evaluation methods in the social, non-profit sector are very under-developed.

At the macroeconomic level, assessing the added value generated by these schemes using traditional economic tools is problematic. At the microeconomic level, evaluation is hampered by the lack of financial measures, such as return on equity, which are widely used in the private sector. Measures of operational efficiency – such as patient throughput – developed in the public sector are likely to miss the value of the benefits created by small innovative organisations.

The difficulties these schemes have in evaluating their success is more than a mere technicality. If they are to make a case for taking a large role in social welfare they will have to persuade politicians and the public that they are delivering value for money.

Permanence and succession

As an organisation becomes more mature and established it confronts new challenges. Perhaps the most pressing challenges when it reaches to top of the curve are how to secure its permanence and an orderly management succession.

Businesses rarely remain small while being genuinely innovative. Innovative businesses tend either to fail, grow or be bought by a larger business. This last route often also solves the issue of management succession. By becoming part of a larger business a small organisation gets access to a wider pool of management talent. As yet social organisations lack such an exit route: there is no market for takeovers to allow a small project to become part of a larger organisation.

One route might be for social organisations to develop a strategic partnership with large companies which might anchor the project. Another route might involve a closer relationship with the state. A durable service contract with the state might provide the best guarantee of stability and permanence for many of these organisations.

Learning from failure

As well as policies to promote success we need policies to minimise the costs of failure. An entrepreneurial sector of the economy must have a high failure rate. There is an element of risk involved in entrepreneurship which is quite alien to the public sector. People must try out a new idea, quite possibly fail, learn from their failure and then try again. But in the social sector, where reputation and probity matter so much failure is often punished harshly. An organisation which runs into financial difficulties often finds it difficult to get new sources of funding. An entrepreneur who founds an organisation which then runs into trouble might find it difficult to find work again. To create a more vibrant socially entrepreneurial sector we need to devise ways for people to experiment and to fail, without being written off. Ideally we need ways to support social entrepreneurs through peaks and troughs just as the best banks support innovative small businesses.

Conclusions

Entrepreneurial social organisations are driven to grow. But as they grow they often run into a range of management obstacles which can thwart their growth or lead to their failure. If social entrepreneurs and their partners were better able to understand these pressures they would be in a better position to overcome them or avoid them.

Public policy issues

How we can create more, successful social entrepreneurs

Social entrepreneurs are developing solutions to some of our most intractable social problems. They generate social capital out of virtually nothing and create new services from scratch. Yet there is only a certain amount they can achieve acting alone. Their great potential is in promoting collaborative solutions to social problems which help to bring together the community and users with the public and private sectors. Social entrepreneurs do not seek to displace or replace the traditional welfare state; they do seek to change it. Getting the right relationship between the public sector and social entrepreneurs is vital.

Social welfare should still be one of our main yardsticks of social progress. A society should be judged by how well it manages to look after its most vulnerable and disadvantaged members. In an increasingly competitive global economy, the economies that will succeed are those that will make best use of all their human capital and assets, while keeping taxes down and restraining public expenditure. The health of the entire economy, including the private sector, in part depends upon innovation in the public sector to create more efficient and effective social services.

Public policy for social innovation cannot be a policy for the state alone. It has to be a policy for creating alliances between social entrepreneurs, the public sector and private companies. We need to create a larger, more vibrant body of social entrepreneurs, within and outside the public sector. We need to find ways to identify, collect and disseminate best practice. Even large organisations can be transformed by ideas generated locally in small office branches or laboratories. Socially entrepreneurial organisations are like social test beds. They offer rare opportunities to conduct practical research and development of social policies. We need to find ways of leveraging the lessons learned in these organisations by transferring their best practice to the public sector.

The private sector can play a vital role in this. Large companies are likely to become increasingly concerned with the 'public policy' aspects of their operations. The best large companies recognise that they are social as well as commercial organisations. However, many companies have yet to find the right channels to route their social interests. Helping to promote social entrepreneurship would be an obvious way forward for the private sector. Not only would the private sector – both large and small companies – have skills to offer, but companies would also stand to benefit from the lessons of entrepreneurship that would emerge from their social partners.

A public policy to promote social entrepreneurship will emerge from a combination of factors as set out in Figure 6 (on page 108): self-help among social entrepreneurs; private sector partnerships with large, small and medium sized companies; state policy at a local, national and European level.

Social entrepreneurs and self-help

One of the main problems facing social entrepreneurs is their isolation and atomisation. They need wider networks to share ideas and spread best practice. Their isolation makes them less efficient than they could be, because often each individual project attempts to come up with its own solutions to problems without knowing how other schemes have tackled the same issue. A Social Entrepreneurs' Network would have several attractions as a way of overcoming this isolation. It could help collect and disseminate best practice. It would provide a forum for debate and ideas. Through it, entrepreneurs could share contacts and links with companies. It could provide a jobs market of sorts, with projects swapping staff or conducting joint training exercises.

A first step could be to promote twinning agreements between schemes in different parts of the country. Such arrangements could lead to staff and client exchanges which would deepen relationships and understanding. It is also possible to imagine supportive financial relationships developing.

A second step would be to encourage franchising. Kaleidoscope for instance could franchise its expertise in drug treatment programmes to other schemes around the country dealing with drug dependency.

A third step would be to create a computer Intranet to link social entrepreneurs. An Intranet is a secure computer communications system that operates rather like a small version of the Internet and the World Wide Web, to which it would be linked. Each project linked to the Intranet would have at least one terminal and a home page on which it would post information about its activities. The Social Entrepreneurs' Intranet would allow projects to share information and ideas about management, funding, regulations and so on. It would also provide the basis for a fledgling jobs exchange. It could become an invaluable research and communications tool for projects which all too often are isolated from people involved in similar activities. The link to the Internet would also serve as a tool for users. With more business being done over the Internet it could also link projects into the mainstream world of on-line business.

A fourth step would be to build upon the Intranet network to create a Centre for Social Entrepreneurs, which would provide a physical presence and focus for meetings, conferences and courses. The centre could provide social entrepreneurs with services such as marketing and management consultancy support, as well as research and help with funding bids. It could also develop a training and teaching arm. One possibility could be a virtual university, using the Intranet, to conduct distance learning for both staff and clients. Another would be to team up with a management college to create a professional qualification for Social Entrepreneurship – an MBA tailored to the needs of social entrepreneurs. Such a centre could provide services for public sector managers and private sector executives concerned with social programmes. At its most ambitious it could become a national centre for public sector management, tasked with the job of promoting best practice in social management and entrepreneurship.

Private sector partnerships
The priority for the private sector should be to deepen its relationship with social entrepreneurs by developing more lasting strategic partnerships. Business in the Community, which has already done much useful work, would be an important focus for encouraging companies to think strategically about their social policies. That could involve several steps.

First, chief executives and senior staff in large companies could mentor and counsel senior staff in social projects. This would provide social entrepreneurs with a sounding board and guidance for addressing significant strategic issues as well as giving them access to a wider business network. A parallel scheme could twin social entrepreneurs with organisational entrepreneurs within large companies. Organisational entrepreneurs, who are seeking to create new business units or new management styles, often run into many of the obstacles of which social entrepreneurs complain.

Figure 6. Policies to promote social innovation

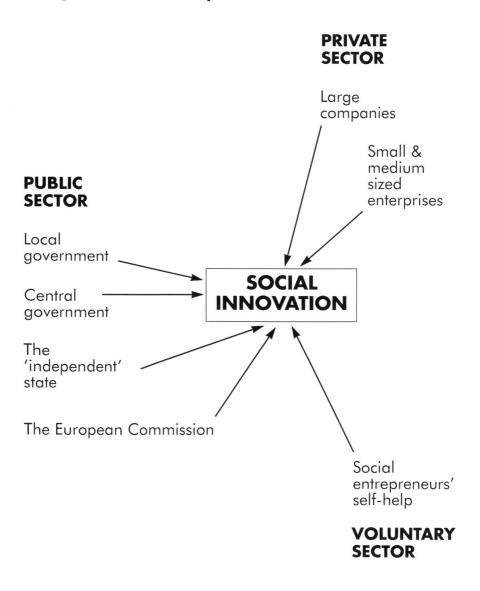

Second, corporations, especially large ones, should develop longer term joint-ventures and funding arrangements with social projects, with the aim of promoting innovation and entrepreneurship. At the moment companies provide secondees, services in kind, unwanted equipment and the like. But much of this involvement is still relatively hand-to-mouth.

Third, companies could provide social entrepreneurs with important skills and resources. Companies are at the leading edge of developing Intranets for instance. This expertise could be made available to social entrepreneurs seeking to set up their own Intranet.

Fourth, the private sector should consider what role it might play in providing start-up and growth finance for social entrepreneurs. Business in the Community has created a loan fund which might provide the basis for a Social Entrepreneurs' fund, which could be run in collaboration with a large bank or 3i, the venture capital house. If a set of corporate sponsors develops a close, committed, long term relationship with a scheme it should be possible for the scheme to use these relationships as financial assets, as security to borrow funds.

Fifth, companies could eventually provide an important exit route for projects which have grown to maturity. Once a project has become more established it could be formally linked to a large company as a related or associated company or as a joint-venture partner. The private sector needs to play a role in creating the forms of hybrid corporate structures that are needed for entrepreneurial social organisations which are both public and private, commercial and charitable. Indeed corporations may have much to learn from structures which are both commercial and social.

Social entrepreneurs and the public sector

Social entrepreneurs will be a vital source of new ideas and management methods for the public sector. If social entrepreneurs are completely separated from the state, they will be marginalised.

Social entrepreneurs criticise the public sector for an alarming mixture of cumbersome bureaucracy and capricious changeability. Yet a public sector that was too homogeneous, armed with a single, directional policy for the social sector would be almost as bad. It would be a mistake for the state to adopt a blanket policy for the voluntary sector. A policy aimed at promoting social innovation and entrepreneurship needs to be discriminating, without falling into the trap of 'picking winners'.

Local government
All the schemes profiled in this report have been deeply influenced by local government policies. All have evolved more productive, trusting relationships with local government as policies have gradually developed, with a culture of contracting out allowing more of a role for social experimentation. The most persistent criticism social entrepreneurs make of local government is its disruptive changeability. It would be worthwhile finding ways to overcome this, perhaps by adopting twinning arrangements, in which a dedicated department of local government becomes responsible for relations with the voluntary sector. This would allow voluntary organisations to form a relationship with a single department, which could become their voice within local government. Staff could be swapped between the council and schemes. Longer term relationships could be built up. This department would be responsible for the council's policy for commissioning work from social entrepreneurs. Such a policy would be promoted by further development of contracting out to include a wider range of services.

The national state
Several measures could be taken by central government to make more of the role of social entrepreneurs.

First, it should focus on developing funding mechanisms. The creation of the Single Regeneration Budget has made life a great deal simpler. The contract culture in health and community care has benefitted many entrepreneurial social organisations. It was widely feared that the shift to contracting out would marketise relations between purchasers and providers and introduce new sources of instability. However early evidence suggests that the contract has become the focus for dialogue and negotiation, which has helped to create a more open, co-operative attitude towards service provision.

Second, the state should help to create a wider network of social entrepreneurs by providing funds to create an Intranet and a Centre for Social Entrepreneurs.

Third, the state should review its regulation of the social sector. Social entrepreneurs are over-regulated by a system which is both onerous and complex. The government should create a simpler, de-regulated corporate structure for entrepreneurial social organisations which combine commercial and charitable work. Such structures exist in Italy, Belgium and the Netherlands. A simple, common corporate form would reduce bureaucracy, increase flexibility and ease governance and management. Social organisations which adopted this hybrid form would have to conform to much more stringent rules of disclosure to ensure that their commercial and charitable finances were being kept separate. Government policy towards small and medium sized enterprises should encompass social organisations seeking to promote collaboration between like minded, similar sized organisations within the same local economy.

Fourth, the government should review its fiscal policy to examine whether it could be used to promote social entrepreneurship, for instance by helping to promote joint-ventures between private companies and social organisations. Some of the spending companies use for this purpose could be given favourable tax treatment.

The quasi-independent state

By the 'quasi-independent state' we mean a growing fringe of state activities which are done at arms length under contract to the central state, including trust hospitals and opted out and locally managed schools.

Locally managed schools and trust hospitals, which have control over their budgets, will increasingly need to learn entrepreneurial skills to develop new services and forms of funding. There should be a growing overlap between social entrepreneurs in the voluntary sector and social entrepreneurs within the independent sector of the state. Schools, universities and hospitals could be twinned with social organisations, to help share costs and develop staff. As these organisations gain more freedom from the central state, they could exploit opportunities for creating local welfare networks combining education, health and social services. In some areas these local welfare and education services could have a significant impact on the local service economy.

Europe

Social entrepreneurship in Britain is increasingly influenced by the policies of the European Union, for example through its pathways funding initiative. Many social entrepreneurs find Brussels a dauntingly distant and unfamiliar place to deal with. There would be great merit then in devising ways to help social entrepreneurs in Britain to bid for EU funds. In addition there are measures which the British government should be urging upon the EU, including simplifying funding procedures, providing a hybrid legal form for social organisations across Europe and facilitating more research in the value of social entrepreneurship across the EU.

Next steps
The steps to social innovation

Social entrepreneurs will help us address our most pressing social problems. But they will only flourish amid the right environment, which will be created largely by the government and the private sector. The process of creating such an environment can start now with ten simple practical steps that will start to create more social entrepeneurs.

1. Social entrepreneurs need to lead the way with schemes for self-help, particularly by promoting local, national and international twinning arrangements between projects to share ideas, contacts and staff.

2. A group of social entrepreneurs led by Andrew Mawson is developing a proposal called '2,000 by 2,000'. The aim of the plan is to create and encourage a body of 2,000 social entrepreneurs by the turn of the century. The schemes they run would then be a local focus for the Millennium celebrations. The '2,000 by 2,000' project would be funded by lottery money. It would create a momentum behind the idea of social entrepreneurship which could provide the basis for further developments such as a Social Entrepreneurs Network. It would give the idea of social entrepreneurship national recognition. These schemes could work in tandem with other important initiatives.

3. The Department of National Heritage should fund research into the feasibility of creating a national Centre for Social Entrepreneurship and a Social Entrepreneurs Inranet. This scheme should also involve large communications and computer companies such as BT and Cable and Wireless. Lord Michael Young, of the Institute for Community Studies, has led the way floating several ideas for centres to promote social entrepreneurship. Anita Roddick's New Academy of Business, which aims to teach ethical business practices, has already developed some of the tools that would be useful.

4. The Department of the Environment should fund local studies and pilot projects which would test the merits of creating local welfare networks, involving locally managed schools, hospitals and welfare services. These networks could be the forerunners of much more developed localised welfare alliances which could in time play a much larger role in local welfare provision. The Single Regeneration Budget could be used to fund the development of such local networks, would build local alliances and improve the capacity of local welfare systems to learn and adapt to change.

5. The Department of the Environment and the Cabinet Office should fund research into the feasibility of creating a national Lessons Learned Unit for the public sector. This unit would augment the Audit Commission and other supervisory bodies which are mainly concerned with accounting for how public money is spent. The Lessons Learned Unit would focus on collecting, interpreting and disseminating examples of best practices in public sector management, especially the development of a contract culture in the public sector.

6. The government should embark on an urgent overhaul of corporate law as it applies to these organisations. The legal structures available to social organisations are unnecessarily cumbersome and complex. A starting point for this would be a review of ownership and legal structures available to social enterprises in Europe.

114

7. Business in the Community should lead a group of large and small companies in an assessment of how their long term relationships with social organisations could be developed. One practical step would be to develop twinning arrangements, to twin social entrepreneurs either with chief executives or with younger organisational entrepreneurs within the business. This would help to link social entrepreneurs into mainstream business.

8. The Department of Trade and Industry should sponsor pilot schemes that would help to create, perhaps via Training and Enterprise Councils, the relationship between social organisations and local networks of small businesses. Social entrepreneurs should be included within the small and medium sized business policy thinking of the DTI, including the schemes for corporate support that it funds.

9. The government should designate a clutch of social entrepreneurs around the country, perhaps 100, which could be the test bed for new policy ideas such as job training allowances, job search programmes, health contracts, educational entitlements. This would be akin to creating a national social policy research laboratory. It would provide a much needed way of systematically testing ideas and policies before launching them on the public sector as a whole.

10. An important aim should be to help more social entrepreneurs make it from start-up into growth and on to maturity. As this report has made clear, entrepreneurs need different kinds of help at different points in this cycle. Social entrepreneurs should be given subsidised access to business advice and consultancy to help them acquire the skills they need, by allowing them to use the 'know-how' schemes the DTI already has in place to help small and medium sized enterprises to develop.